The
Restoration
Project

The Restoration Project

A Benedictine Path to Wisdom, Strength, and Love

Christopher H. Martin

Forward Movement
Cincinnati, Ohio

**Forward
Movement**
www.forwardmovement.org

*Restore us, O L*ORD *God of hosts;*
show the light of your countenance
and we shall be saved.
—Psalm 80:18

For Chloe, Harper, and Simon
and in memory of Br. Paul Wessinger, SSJE

What Readers Are Saying

How can we know the way? Christopher Martin writes with tested wisdom about our need for restoration if we are to become what we already are. He is as conversant with Benedict of Nursia and Bernard of Clairvaux as he is about abuse, addiction, and the tedium of making mistakes. Christopher is a master weaver of poetry and art, ancient and new. He gives very shrewd spiritual direction when we stumble because of the fear or aggression we are loath to face. Some of his compelling stories will make your eyes twinkle; others will lance a wound, your wound. How countercultural—his writing about the steps toward humility, admittedly "a long climb,"—yet something so helpful and hopeful, and which he models. Christopher helps us settle into stillness so that we can really and finally listen to God.

— Br. Curtis Almquist SSJE
The Society of Saint John the Evangelist
Cambridge, Massachusetts

I love the book! I have told friends about it already, and they are excited to read it as well. When Our Potters House bookstore reopens, I will make sure it "hits" our shelves.

— Mike Little
Church of the Saviour,
Washington, D.C.

I n *The Restoration Project*, Father Christopher Martin has applied ancient Benedictine wisdom to the twenty-first-century spiritual journey and embattled post-modern Church. He has rediscovered (maybe re-presented) habits for living that are radically changing the character of Christian community and wonderfully enriching the lives of the people of God. Reader be forewarned: the ideas in this book may change your life. They have changed mine!

— THE RT. REV. J. SCOTT BARKER
EPISCOPAL BISHOP OF NEBRASKA

C hristopher Martin not only does the difficult work of translating Benedict's thoughts from the fifth century to our world but also has created a process in community for putting Benedict's teachings into practice. Altogether, Christopher has created a useful tool for Christian living. If you and some friends embark on the journey laid out in *The Restoration Project*, God will meet you and guide you into a life of authenticity, peace, and joy.

— THE RT. REV. MARC ANDRUS
EPISCOPAL BISHOP OF THE
DIOCESE OF CALIFORNIA

What Readers Are Saying

Table of Contents

Chapter 7

Introduction

I love my church. St. Paul's is a hidden jewel in the heart of the largest town in Marin County in the Bay Area of California. The outside of the building is a non-descript, pale grey stucco, but the inside is stunning. It was built in 1869 in a style called Carpenter Gothic. This means it has the shape and furnishings of an ancient village church in England, but it is constructed out of wood, not stone. As a result, it has the dignity and depth of tradition combined with the warmth of well-aged local wood.

Even more than the building, I love what the space brings out in people. It is a long, narrow church with the altar some distance from the front pew. When the community sits to worship, nearly everyone faces to the west, toward the altar, toward what can feel like God. As the leader of the worship service, I am frequently facing the east and looking into the faces of the people. I know nearly everyone well, so I recognize that when they are in this space in worship, any semblance of a mask falls away. The faces I see are open, vulnerable, and yearning. There are tears, there are smiles, and there is often an expression suggesting the person is focused on some new life that is just coming into being.

As beautiful and moving as these moments in worship are, they are only moments. I know all of us will soon go out into a world that will do almost nothing to encourage what we experience in these sacred moments in church. If, like me, you want to be a good person, to be known and loved in a spiritual community you trust, and to have an intimate sense of God's presence in your everyday life, then church on Sundays is not enough. Jesus warns us that the cares of the world can choke out our love of God. We need something during the week to keep our love of God alive. A church building can't be the only religious structure we have.

This book is a guide for keeping God at the center of our lives by using one of the most ancient and reliable structures, Saint Benedict's twelve steps of humility. While *The Rule of Saint Benedict* is often embraced by monastic communities, this book applies the saint's ancient wisdom to the daily lives of those of us who are not monks or nuns. As a way to guide you through the twelve steps, I connect the process of spiritual growth to the story of the restoration of *The Last Supper,* the famous painting by Leonardo da Vinci. Imagine that your soul is like the face of one of the disciples before the painting was restored: your soul is fundamentally beautiful, created by the hand of the master, but it needs some restoration work so that you may reveal the God-given beauty of your soul to the world. If you would like to see what the faces of the apostles looked like before the restoration, just look at the cover of this book.

This book and the proposed spiritual practices emerged from ceaseless experiments to help people bring their Sunday experiences of God into their weekday lives. Several years ago I began sharing my discoveries with friends and colleagues around the country. Our conversations grew into The Restoration Project, a nationwide movement of churches creating vibrant experiences for people to explore and claim their faith during the week. We are an "open source" community sharing with each other ways to create and maintain a variety of structures that hold us in the love of Christ every moment of our lives. The core of our movement is a simple structure for small groups. I describe these Discipleship Groups throughout the book.

Whoever you are, from whatever walk of life, you are welcome to join our community. What binds us together is a common desire to follow Jesus through a shared set of practices. We build upon our love of worship by adding twenty minutes of prayer each day and by regularly serving the poor in our communities. On the sure foundation of these simple practices, we hope to grow and mature in our shared life in Christ. We are not a community of experts or of the ultra-holy. Some of us are brand new to the church and to Christianity, while others are church veterans open to a new thing. I encourage you to read this book as an invitation to join The Restoration Project.

— CHRISTOPHER H. MARTIN

CHAPTER 1

The Restoration of a Masterpiece

Leonardo da Vinci loved faces. If he saw a face in the streets of Milan, Italy that fascinated him, he would take the day off from painting his famous masterpiece, *The Last Supper*, so that he could follow that person and study the face. At the end of the day, Leonardo would return to his house and stay up deep into the night, sketching from memory. Details from those sketches would find their way to his painting.[1] Leonardo wanted his masterpiece to reveal to the viewer real people in every detail.

No one has ever been better than Leonardo at capturing in paint a human soul. Just two years before he began *The Last Supper*, he completed *The Lady with an Ermine*. In this piece, a beautiful young woman holds a small animal and looks to her left; she appears to be caught in mid-conversation. This painting from about 1490 is considered by many art historians the first European painting to capture the motions of a person's mind, the moment of transition from thought to expression.

Only a few years after completing *The Last Supper*, Leonardo finished his most well-known painting, the *Mona Lisa*. From the beginning, people were stunned by the verisimilitude of the painting, claiming one could almost see the veins pulsing under the skin of her neck. Her watchful eyes and enigmatic smile evoke complex, unresolved emotions—similar to our experiences with real people in our lives today and perhaps even from the deepest reflections on our selves.

Most of us don't look at human faces with quite the same intensity as Leonardo. That would be rude. I was once made to stare deeply into another's face, and the moment has haunted me ever since. The instructor paired us off in a college class and asked us to sit cross-legged on the floor about two feet away from our partner. We were directed to look into each other's eyes and ask, over and over, "who are you, really?" As the exercise progressed, I became increasingly anxious. I could find no word or picture to answer the question. I knew, of course, that I was male, a college student, and the son of Vicki and Peter, but the repetition of the question begged for an even deeper response. Who am I, really?

I have come to believe the answers to all the hardest questions are found in the scriptures. The Bible has the capacity to address the unanswerable questions. The answers may be mysterious and paradoxical, they may appear as a question or as a truth we would prefer not to believe, but the answers are there, and we can rely on them.

Scripture presents a variety of ways to understand who we really are, but one of the most powerful is found early in the Bible. The first chapter of Genesis gives us the deep truth of the origins of all things. Faithful reflection on that first chapter teaches us that God created everything out of nothing—and out of love (Genesis 1:1). It teaches us that, in God's original intention, everything was created "very good" (Genesis 1:31). And, mysteriously, scripture teaches us that human beings, male and female, were created in the image and likeness of God (Genesis 1:26).

Our souls, created in the image and likeness of God, are like the faces in *The Last Supper*. When the painting was completed in 1498, the thirteen figures were every bit as lively and compelling as the *Mona Lisa*. But soon after, the painting began to deteriorate because of an innovative but unstable material used for the base. Within fifty years, the masterpiece was described as "miraculous" but "half-ruined."[2] The ensuing centuries were not kind to the painting. It underwent seven restoration attempts, each of which only served to cover and distort the original. Further, the French leader Napoleon Bonaparte turned the room that housed the painting into a horse stable, and the Allies accidently bombed the building in World War II. Pollution and grime of the air in the nineteenth and twentieth centuries accumulated on the surface. By the late 1950s, the painting was a disappointing, dark blur.

The turning point for the painting came in 1978, when science, the technology of art restoration, and the state of Leonardo studies had all progressed far enough that people were confident they could, as far as possible, restore *The Last Supper*. A master restorer, Pinin Brambilla Barcilon, was given the authority, the time, and the resources she needed to do the best work possible.

I invite you to imagine that your soul is like one of the faces of *The Last Supper*. Because you are God's beloved child, you were fashioned with at least the same amount of care Leonardo gave to his great portraits. Because God made you in God's own image, you have within you the capacity to be good, beautiful, and true. You are invited to show the world the divine image in you.

This comparison of the restoration of *The Last Supper* and our souls has good news and bad news for us. The good news is that we were created lively and beautiful by the hand of the master. God created us in God's own beautiful image. We don't need to become something or someone else. From the Christian point of view, there is no such thing as the proverbial "self-made man." God made us, and our only work is, paradoxically, to become what we already are.

There is more good news. We know what it looks like when a human being perfectly shows forth the image and likeness of God. The climax of our scriptural story is that, in the fullness of time, God sent God's only son, who "is the exact imprint of God's very being" (Hebrews 1:3). If we look to Jesus, we see what it means to be perfectly good, truthful, and beautiful. We may have only a vague sense of what it means for us to show forth the image in which we were created, but when we look to Jesus, when we remember and reflect on his life, we can be confident that we are gazing on a human life without fault or blemish. It is as though, in a painting otherwise decayed and defaced, one face is miraculously complete.

The bad news is that so much in our lives has obscured our God-given beauty. The integrity of the likeness to God has broken apart; the foundation has not been firm. We have tried to fix things and often made them worse, and the environment in which we live can be toxic, violent, and aggressive. Whether you call it abuse, addiction, mistakes, or sin, all is not well, and all is not as it should be. We present to the world a likeness that is a corruption of what the Master intended. We need restoration if we are to become what God intended—and what we already are beneath the decay and grime.

The faces in *The Last Supper* were not uniform in their deterioration. Some, like Thomas, retained their expressiveness and, as it turned out, were not that far from Leonardo's original intention. For others, like John, ninety percent of the face had been lost, leaving only a pale shadow of the original. Right now, you and I are somewhere in that continuum, still able to reflect the beautiful hand of the Master yet showing a face far less good, true, or beautiful than God intended.

It took Barcilon and her team twenty-two years of careful, determined work to complete their restoration project. She wrote that "each day proved a new and engrossing experience, but one inevitably grounded in caution and reflection, confirmation, and consultation."[3] It was not always easy. Their process required time, persistence, endurance, teamwork, and some measure of skill. Our process of restoration requires nothing less.

In order to embark on the restoration of our souls, we need help. We need help with our thoughts, and we need help with our behavior. This book gives you an internal spiritual structure to help you orient your thoughts throughout the week and through the course of your long climb. This internal structure comes from prayerful reflection on an ancient and reliable spiritual tradition in western Christianity, the way of Saint Benedict. He was the founder of the western monastic tradition and developed a twelve-step process to spiritual restoration.

Born in the 500s to a noble family outside of Rome, Benedict left his home as a young man and became a hermit. Within some years, stories of his holiness had spread, and people came to him to ask him to become their spiritual master, or abbot. As part of his role as abbot, Benedict devised a short Rule of Life. It seems clear that he used material inherited from previous fathers and mothers of the faith but added his own spirit of balance, moderation, and practical reason.

From the tone of the *Rule*, the man seems sober, practical, and stern, not at all an unearthly mystic, although he is capable of a few moments of compelling beauty. The Twelve Steps of Humility are the heart of his *Rule*. The chapter in which he explains the twelve steps, which I've included in the back of this book, is the longest in the *Rule*.

When he writes about the steps of humility, Saint Benedict describes an image of a ladder with twelve rungs. This is based on Benedict's interpretation of Jacob's dream found in the Book of Genesis. Perhaps you know the story: the patriarch Jacob flees his home after outwitting his older brother Esau. After a time he takes a rest. The story continues that "he dreamed that there was a ladder set up on the earth, the top of it reaching to heaven; and the angels of God were ascending and descending on it" (Genesis 28:12). Along with most of the church through history, Benedict views Jacob's dream as a gift from God that gives us a way to God. Benedict imagines that the ladder Jacob saw has twelve rungs or steps (The Rule of Saint Benedict, 7:6). This book is a user's guide to these twelve steps that can help us as we seek an intimate encounter with God.[4]

The prologue to Saint Benedict's *Rule* concludes with a few sentences that seem to capture much of the man. He writes,

"We hope to set down nothing harsh, nothing burdensome… The good of all concerned, however, may prompt us to a little strictness in order to amend faults and to safeguard love. Do not be daunted immediately by fear and run away from the road that leads to salvation. It is bound to be narrow at the outset. But as we progress in this way of life and in faith, we shall run on the path of God's commandments, our hearts overflowing with the inexpressible delight of love" (THE RULE OF SAINT BENEDICT, *Prologue*: 46-49).

Over the next thousand years, Saint Benedict's *Rule* was popular in Western Europe as a way of life for those who wished to make Christian vows of poverty, chastity, and obedience. Even the lives of those outside the monastery walls were changed for the better by the teachings, the witness, and especially the prayers of those inside. *The Book of Common Prayer*, the core document of my own Christian denomination, The Episcopal Church, relies heavily on the *Rule* of Saint Benedict. The original architect of *The Book of Common Prayer*, Thomas Cranmer, used the prayers and rhythm of life of the Benedictines to create, in the common language of the people, an essentially Benedictine way of life for an ordinary person. For example, he took the seven daily prayer services of the monks and nuns and condensed them into two—Morning and Evening Prayer.

Although Benedictine sensibility is a part of many Western Christian denominations, there are few guides or commentaries on the twelve steps of humility— especially for people who aren't monks and nuns. I'm not sure why that is. What I do know is that I was saved by the Twelve Steps of Humility. In the midst of a season of deep disorientation and pain, I found Michael Casey's *A Guide to Living in the Truth*.

Casey is a monk in the Benedictine tradition with a doctorate in medieval theology. His book is a commentary for today's monks and nuns and is rooted in solid academic research. Some parts are a bit dry, but there are also parts that, for me, leapt off the page and spoke precisely to my spiritual state. In a time of deep disorientation, the twelve steps as unpacked by Casey gave me a reliable map so that I could, if only faintly, discern God's presence in my pain and so stay faithful. It showed me the path of love and hope, even if I did not always follow it.

Because it was so helpful for me, I was eager to share its wisdom with others. But I found that the words and ideas did not easily translate to individuals' lives and ways of understanding things. My background had made Casey's book accessible to me. I had been to seminary and have always had a passion for ancient spiritual wisdom. For years I had close friendships with monks and nuns, and their struggles and ways of being were familiar to me. When I tried to share Casey's book with others, I found it didn't resonate with them; it didn't sing for them the way it sang for me.

In the decade since I first read Casey, I have read and reflected on many of the books on the twelve steps of humility. I have had conversations about the steps and have taught classes on them. Above all, I have tried to live by them as best as I can. This book reflects this journey and offers one way of beginning to walk a life-saving path for yourself.

Saint Benedict suggests that his *Rule* is for beginners, and he begins and ends with the suggestion that some saints have progressed far beyond what he describes. Without the benefit of experience, readers might think that if they followed the instructions in the *Rule* for a year or two, they would soon be ready for the next great spiritual thing. In practice, people have found that the *Rule*, and in particular the Twelve Steps of Humility, are sufficient for a lifetime. The *Rule* may only encompass Twelve Steps, but it is, for almost all of us, a long climb.

Furthermore, the way of Saint Benedict is not a solo journey; it is always pursued in relationship with others. So while you can use this book just by yourself, I intend it as an invitation to join a national movement with the same name as this book, The Restoration Project. The movement is open to all Christians who hunger for spiritual depth in community. What binds us together is a set of classic practices that have proven to be effective ways to grow wise, spiritually strong, and loving.

The most important structure of The Restoration Project community is Discipleship Groups. These are small groups that meet regularly, often every week or every other week. Each meeting begins with some time of silence, an expression of a common intention to seek God through Christ, and then a recitation of seven vows. An explanation of these seven vows is integrated into the beginning chapters of this book. (The full liturgy for a Discipleship Group can be found at the back of this book).

Just as Saint Benedict's monastery provided the best context for nuns and monks to follow his spiritual wisdom, so Discipleship Groups provide the best context I know for ordinary Christians who desire to be held in love while they die to their old selves and are reborn in Christ. We all need help. Without loving structure, our spiritual growth will stall, and we will never become the person God created us to be. We each have been given unique gifts and were created to complete a particular piece of God's work. The Restoration Project, like Benedict's Twelve Steps of Humility, is intended as a reliable and tested structure for revealing to the world the beautiful soul God created in each of us.

CHAPTER 2

Foundational Habits:
Two Personal Steps

1. Keeping Watch
2. Desiring God Above All

A team of young professionals—all at the top of their classes—stood with Barcilon in 1980 on the first day of restoring *The Last Supper*. These passionate young people would draw on a range of skills to help reveal the beauty intended by Leonardo. The team decided to begin on the right side of the painting around the clustered figures of Matthew, Thaddeus, and Simon.

Unlike in many of the previous restoration attempts, the team was not going to repaint. Instead they would focus their energies on cleaning. They were going to use specially designed solvents and fixates to address the dirt and grime. To guide the work, they relied on microscopes, a powerful magnifying lens, and various lighting techniques. They worked with a hygrometer, a tool that uses electronic sensors, x-ray, infrared, and ultraviolet technologies to determine the state of the painting and its environment. They coordinated with a local laboratory to analyze paint chips to identify which layers of paint came from the hand of Leonardo—and which were from later repainting restorations.[5] Every member of the team had years of experience in restoration of other paintings, all in preparation for this, their greatest challenge.

Like the professional restorers, we too can acquire skills, practices, and attitudes to ensure our best work as we approach the restoration of our spiritual selves. Now is the time to begin the serious work of becoming who we are. The first four steps of humility are habits that over time help us to become the spiritual equivalents of passionate professionals. These habits give us the best possible opportunity to reveal, by God's grace, the hand of the master creator to the world.

The first two of these four steps are personal disciplines we cultivate within ourselves. As individual practices, we must learn to keep watch, which is the ability to remember at all times that God is with us. We must also desire God above all, which means simply that we begin to follow the Great Commandment, loving God with our whole heart, mind, soul, and strength and loving our neighbor as ourselves.

Step One:
Keeping Watch

He guards himself at every moment…
— THE RULE OF SAINT BENEDICT, 7:12

"Are you there, God?"

If there is any question that is as deep, disconcerting, and unanswerable as "who am I, really?" it must be the question of God's presence. I often ask, in many and various ways, about people's favorite passage of scripture. More often than not, it is a passage that reassures us that God is in fact with us and that God knows us and cares for us. "You have searched me out and known me," we say with Psalm 139. "Though I walk through the valley of the shadow of death, I shall fear no evil; for you are with me," we say with Psalm 23. "I am with you always, to the end of the age," we hear Jesus say at the end of the Gospel of Matthew (28:20), and we yearn to believe it.

No one feels God's presence all the time, at every moment of his or her life. Even the greatest saints have moments of doubt, uncertainty, and darkness. But saints are those who, over time, are more likely to be aware when God has made Godself known to them. Over time they are the ones who are more likely to shift the question, like Saint Augustine in his *Confessions*. The more he looked back over his life, the more his perspective changed from the question "Where were you, God?" to, "O God, you were there; where was I?"[6]

Benedict's first step repeatedly emphasizes God's presence. For example, he writes, "let him recall that he is always seen by God in heaven, that his actions everywhere are in God's sight and are reported by angels at every hour" (THE RULE OF SAINT BENEDICT, 7:13). Benedict imagines that God is everywhere, around us at every moment.

One way to understand this is to see God like the experience of water when we scuba dive, a constant presence offering both great beauty and some measure of peril. Almost anyone can learn to scuba dive. The modern equipment is intuitive, well designed, and reliable. One can learn to be a safe diver in a matter of days, and by learning to scuba dive, we gain access to some of the most breathtaking sights in our world. But the water also contains an element of danger that no amount of equipment can circumvent. If we rise to the surface too quickly, we can get decompression sickness—the bends. If we don't dive according to plan, we can get lost. If we don't monitor our depth, we can pass out. Diving accidents happen.

But diving accidents don't tend to happen to beginners. After a bit of training, most beginners are attentive and respectful because the newness tends to keep us alert. Accidents happen to people who have been diving for a while without incident and begin to lose their vigilance. Like a good dive instructor, Benedict emphasizes from the beginning that we need to keep watch constantly and over the long term if we wish to make progress. The first step, then, is serious and asks us to take ourselves seriously. It calls us to a life that marks a middle way. We are to be neither flippant and silly nor morose and withdrawn. Instead we are to be watchful, open, and persistent. If we stay watchful, like good divers, we will see rare creatures and have unique adventures without getting hopelessly lost or needlessly hurt.

Benedict also calls us to be like good craftspeople. Throughout his short *Rule* he refers to his monks as "workmen" and his monastery as a "workshop" (THE RULE OF SAINT BENEDICT, 4:78). Mastering any craft takes time, attention, and seriousness of purpose. The people who joined Barcilon had spent years learning the art and craft of restoration. They mastered chemistry, art history, and painting itself. They spent hundreds of hours training their muscles to be steady and reliable. They learned to be attentive, patient, and careful. Serious spiritual growth demands the same virtues of us.

The difference between the craft of the restorers and our craft of spiritual growth is that, at the end of the day, the restorers could put down their brushes and leave the work. The half-restored face of an apostle can wait weeks or months. By contrast we live with our faces all the time. There's nowhere to go from ourselves. Wherever we go, there we are. Now is always the time to be about the work of soul restoration. There is no other time than now to be spiritual.

This first step of keeping watch reminds us that, in the view of the Benedictine tradition, attention to God is not restricted to what we might think of as "spiritual" practices and experiences. One of Benedict's great interpreters, the eleventh-century monk Bernard of Clairvaux, writes that if a monk can't pay attention to his reading of scripture, he should go work in the garden, on his knees, because there in the dirt he can learn the same lesson that scripture teaches, that of humility.[7] Over time, we can learn to do all things with an awareness that God is with us, from gardening to making dinner, from shuttling children to writing an email.

Can we picture, as we write to another, that the words we type are an extension of God's care for the world? If, in our time of prayer, we become aware of God's subtle presence, are we able to maintain some palpable connection to the still, small, elusive voice even as we face the screen? The work and practice of the twelve steps allows the restoration of God's grace to slowly seep into more and more of our lives.

In this first step, we are invited to be like a couple expecting their first child. When my wife Chloe and I first found out she was pregnant, our lives subtly shifted. We continued to care for our house, see our friends, and go to work, but our relationship to each of those things changed. Over time our house changed. We redecorated a room, and parenting books started stacking up on our bedside tables. While Chloe was pregnant, we ate and drank differently. Our work began to seem a little less important, and we didn't hesitate to leave for doctor's appointments and parenting classes. My thoughts during the day shifted. On my commute to work I wondered if my car was safe enough to carry a baby.

Similarly, entering into these twelve steps of humility means nurturing a sense of attention and expectation that can change the texture of our lives. If we are watchful in the present moment, perhaps we will cut down the amount of time we spend online with our heads in the Internet cloud and spend more time being fully present where our bodies happen to be. Perhaps we will find a small physical reminder of God's presence like a cross for our necks or prayer beads for our pockets. Perhaps we will learn an ancient repetitive prayer like "Lord Jesus Christ, Son of the Living God, have mercy on me, a sinner"[8] and spend a little bit of time each day saying it.

Maybe every now and then we will close the door and say the Lord's Prayer or sit in a few minutes of silence. Perhaps a few books on prayer and the Christian life will start appearing on our bedside tables.

When a baby is coming, the shifts in our lives are fueled by a sense of expectation. Our preparations and our thoughtfulness come from a yearning to meet the baby and have her enter a world in which she can thrive. Likewise our sense of watchfulness, and indeed our progress throughout the twelve steps, will often emerge from our own sense of expectation and yearning for God.

For those of us in liturgical churches, the experience of the season of Advent can be an important help in carving out this sense of expectation. I often think of the liturgical year as a circle around the mystery of God. Each of the seasons in our tradition—Epiphany, Lent, Holy Week, Easter, Ordinary Time, and Advent—gives us a different perspective on the unfathomable mystery at the center of our life. In Advent we are asked to attend most to our own yearning for God to come into our lives and do a new thing. We yearn for God to come to us once again as a baby at Christmas and to appear in our lives now in some new, wonderful way. As we sing together "O Come, O Come, Emmanuel," we are nurturing our desire for God and learning to heed Jesus' repeated admonition to "keep watch!"

Throughout Christian history, constant watchfulness has been viewed as an entire spiritual practice in itself. One follower of Saint Benedict, Saint Romuald, wrote a short, simple Rule in the eleventh century that still governs his order, now called the New Camaldolese. The Rule captures in sweet, homely images the life of a watchful follower of God. Here it is in its entirety:

> Sit in your cell as in paradise. Put the whole world behind you and forget it. Watch your thoughts like a good fisherman watching for fish. The path you must follow is the Psalms—never leave it.
>
> If you have just come to the monastery, and in spite of your good will you cannot accomplish what you want, take every opportunity you can to sing the Psalms in your heart and to understand them with your mind.
>
> And if your mind wanders as you read, do not give up; hurry back and apply your mind to the words once more.
>
> Realize above all that you are in God's presence, and stand there with the attitude of one who stands before the emperor.
>
> Empty yourself completely and sit waiting, content with the grace of God, like the chick who tastes nothing and eats nothing but what his mother brings him.[9]

The watchful chick in Romuald's lovely closing image desires nothing but the food brought by its mother. Our desires are always more complicated than that, and so we are rapidly brought to Benedict's second step.

Step Two:
Desiring God Above All

loves not his own will nor takes pleasure in
the satisfaction of his own desire...

— THE RULE OF SAINT BENEDICT, 7:31

Jesus' great commandment is apparently very simple. We are to "love the Lord our God with our whole heart, mind, soul, and strength...and (our) neighbor as (ourself)" (Matthew 22:36-40). The good news is that we were created to fulfill this commandment. When our love is wholly consumed with the appropriate love of God, neighbor, and self, we are the image and likeness of God, reflecting back God's glory as we are intended to do.

And yet this is generally not our state. Other desires always seem to take higher priority. Sometimes we seem to love chocolate more than God. Other times, sleep, TV, or work supercede God in our lives. The second step of humility asks us to be honest about our priorities. What are we drawn toward? What do we really want and desire?

The simplest Christian formula for a virtuous life comes to us from Saint Augustine. In *City of God* he writes, "hence, as it seems to me, a brief and true definition of virtue is rightly ordered love."[10] He is commenting on the Latin translation of a verse from the Song of Songs where the bride observes that the bridegroom has "ordered love in me" (Song of Solomon 2:4). As is often the case in the Christian tradition, Augustine uses the bridegroom in the Song of Songs to represent Jesus and the bride to represent the human soul. Jesus' work with us is to order our love properly so that, as he commands, the love of God is always first, and the loves of self and neighbor follow.

The Christian idea of rightly ordered love assumes that it is okay to love the things of this world. Some of Augustine's great theological opponents were the Manicheans, who assumed the material world was essentially evil and the task of the truly spiritual was to escape it. Augustine, and the Benedictine tradition that followed him, assume with scripture that the world is "very good" (Genesis 1:31). Evil expresses itself not in love of the world but in our love of worldly objects and ambitions more than God, neighbor, and self. Augustine offers the practical example of a miser who loves his gold more than his children.

This second step of humility asks us to become aware of the way we prioritize what we love, not just in theory but also in practice. Our hearts and minds might tell us one thing, but it is very likely that our behavior is telling the world something else. If we want to know what we love, our best data is to look at our budgets and our schedules. On whom or what are we spending our money and time? Do these decisions reflect our best values?

For all of us, the answer to that last question is "no." We all have places in our lives where we spend an inordinate amount of time, money, and attention, often in ways that are unreflective. A breakthrough for me came several years ago when I was reading an article about micro-targeting in marketing. I had always imagined I had an independent and quirky sense of taste. I had thought the things that I wear, drive, eat, and listen to represent in a significant way who I was as a unique and independent human being. But as I read this article, I realized with a sinking stomach that I fit quite neatly into a kind of metropolitan VW-Starbucks-Banana Republic niche, and that given two or three pieces of information about me, people and computer programs could pretty accurately guess the rest. I believe, because I live in one of the most secular counties in the United States, that the only thing it wouldn't guess about me, given my profile, is that I am Christian. I was left with a dilemma that I continue to struggle with. Does my consumption match my highest Christian values?

My consumption, which I had understood as a place of freedom, turned out to be a kind of trap, with my environment finely tuned to urge me to consume more. And I have been, and continue to be, a willing subject. In short, I am an addict to the culture, far too often allowing culture to determine what I desire. The cost of mindless consuming is that I might soon find myself in a real spiritual wilderness, not unlike the Israelites after leaving Egypt.

> *But they soon forgot his deeds*
> *And did not wait for his counsel.*
>
> *A craving seized them in the wilderness,*
> *And they put God to the test in the desert.*
>
> *He gave them what they asked,*
> *But sent leanness into their soul.*
>
> —Psalm 106:13-15

An ancient practice that can help us detach a bit from our own consumption is to develop a habit of generosity toward God and the poor. The vow in Discipleship Groups reminds us of this practice when we say "by God's grace, I will be a good steward of my money, working toward giving ten percent to the church and those in need, mindful that 'where you treasure is, there your heart will be also' (Matthew 6:21)."

The stakes are high. Our disordered consuming can lead to extraordinary loss. I have a friend who was married to a man with a rapidly accelerating cocaine habit. She told me that one day she looked over at him as they were sitting together on their couch. She realized that as she looked into his eyes, she could no longer see his soul. His desire for cocaine had gradually smothered any visible sign of his divine spark. With a shock and with deep sadness, she knew she had to leave him to keep her own soul alive and not get sucked into his pit. It was as though the last visible vestiges of the hand of the master had crumbled away from the painting.

We are all addicts of something and are all in need of recovery. We all need restoration. The good news is that the power that restores us comes from God, not us. When Augustine writes of "rightly ordered love," he recalls the passage of scripture in which a bride pleads to her bridegroom to "set love in order in me" (Song of Solomon 2:4). The bridegroom acts, and the bride accepts. Likewise, when it comes to our desires for consumption, we must let God do the ordering. We only make ourselves available to God—and then get out of the way.

Two fundamental Christian practices invite God to set love in order in us. Without them, we are likely to stall.

The first is centering prayer. This form of Christian meditation was recovered and then reinterpreted in the 1960s by monks in the Benedictine tradition. They relied on a fourteenth-century English text called *The Cloud of*

Unknowing to develop a simple practice for today's believers. Centering Prayer invites us to sit comfortably in a quiet place with our eyes closed for twenty minutes. During that time we use a short word to ever so gently nudge aside any thought that comes into our minds. That is it. It may sound simple, and it is, but it is not easy to implement in our lives. I have yet to meet anyone for whom it has been smooth sailing. I also have yet to meet anyone who has stuck with it and regretted the time invested in the practice.

There is now great practical wisdom about what happens if you follow the practice faithfully. Thomas Keating, a monk in the Benedictine tradition, is one of the leaders of this movement of centering prayer and wrote a magnificent introduction to the practice in his book, *Open Mind, Open Heart.* He calls the practice "divine therapy,"[11] a way of naming the process of God setting love "in order" in us. There are many layers of this "divine therapy," but for the purposes of this second step of desiring God above all, there is at least one very powerful characteristic. As we sit with our eyes closed, we are receiving no external stimulation and are satisfying none of our bodies' desires. For at least twenty minutes, we do not consume. Further, if a thought comes into our brains, "I want a cookie," at least in the moment, we get to practice letting it go. Centering prayer is a gentle beginning of the practices of fasting, detachment, and restraint, allowing God to set love in order in us. Centering prayer is a regular expression in our daily schedules of our love of God.

Research shows that people who commit at least twenty minutes a day to prayer express a far greater level of satisfaction with their spiritual life than people who commit less time.[12] So, in our Discipleship Groups, we commit to setting aside time regularly for prayer, "praying to God who is in secret" and working toward twenty minutes a day (Matthew 6:6). Through years of teaching, I have found it is helpful to first make a commitment to where you want to pray and when you want to pray, and then figure out what to do in that place and time. It can be a great pleasure to create a sacred, uncluttered space for our daily prayers. I've had students create spaces out of their desks, in their bedrooms, and even out of their closets. I had one student with a home life that was so chaotic, she chose to leave home a little earlier in the morning, park under a favorite tree near work, and then pull a religious icon out of the glove compartment to prop up on the dashboard. For her, as for all of us, the key was finding a time in the day, very often in the morning, to consistently take time to pray.

The other practice to help train our desires toward God is daily reading of scripture. Augustine was one of two main influences on Saint Benedict. The other was the wisdom that came from the Desert Fathers and Mothers in Egypt from the fourth and fifth centuries. People throughout the Mediterranean came to the Egyptian desert to meet these stern yet compassionate people and soon collected their stories and sayings.

Here is an example of one well-known piece of wisdom. In the scriptural tradition, "hardness of heart" is anything that keeps us from God, and "fear of God" is always the first step in a living relationship with God. Fear of God is the fundamental realization that God is God and we are not.

> The nature of water is soft, that of stone is hard; but if a bottle is hung above the stone, allowing the water to fall drop by drop, it wears away the stone. So it is with the word of God; it is soft but our heart is hard, but

the man who hears the word of God often, opens his heart to the fear of God.[13]

A simple practice like praying the Daily Office from *The Book of Common Prayer,* where a few psalms and some short readings are assigned for each day, provides us with a baseline of hearing the Word of God frequently, drop by drop.

One of the great mysteries of the Christian faith is our belief that the Old and New Testaments are a living word, with the capacity to train us in righteousness (2 Timothy 3:16). In a way that is beyond our conscious knowing, the word of God slowly remakes our hearts, slowly puts love in order in us. In Discipleship Groups, we make learning scripture a lifelong project by vowing that "By God's grace, I will read, mark, learn, and inwardly digest[14] the Holy Scriptures, trusting that they are 'inspired by God' for my 'training in righteousness' working toward knowledge of the entire book" (2 Timothy 3:16).

If reading scripture becomes a daily habit, there will be days where it makes sense and speaks to us, and then other days when we won't seem to remember in the very next minute what we just read. Never mind. The practice is to keep showing up, if even for a few minutes, trusting that God's word in scripture restores.

Just as we will never, in this life, achieve some perfect stance of watchfulness, neither will our loves ever be perfectly ordered. Although the daily practice of praying and reading scripture is important, we know that we'll continue the struggle as we gradually grow and mature. At the end of his *Rule,* Benedict calls his work a "little rule that we have written for beginners" (THE RULE OF SAINT BENEDICT, 73:8) and then refers to the Desert Fathers and Mothers as among those who are as close as we can come to perfection. Another story from the desert can put our own struggles in perspective.

> There was a certain elder who had fasted valiantly for fifty years, and he said: I have put out the flames of lust and avarice and vainglory. Abbot Abraham heard about it and came to him asking: Did you really say that? I did, he replied. Then Abbot Abraham said: So you go into your cell, and there is a woman lying on your mat. Can you think that she is not a woman? He said, No, but I fight my thoughts so that I don't touch that woman. Then, said Abbot Abraham, you have not killed fornication. The passion is alive, but it is bound. And now supposing you are on a journey and in the road among the stones and broken pottery you see some gold: can you think of it as if it were like other stones? No, he replied, but I resist my thoughts so that I do not pick it up. The Abbot Abraham said: You see, the passion is alive. But it is bound. Then Abbot Abraham said again: You hear about two brothers, of whom one likes you and the other hates you and speaks evil of you. They come to you: and do you receive them both alike? No, he replied, but I am tormented inside, trying to be just as nice to the one who hates me as I am to the other. Abbot Abraham said: The passions live, then. But in the saints they are only, to some extent, bound.[15]

Our human cravings will never be fully extinguished. The desire for consumption of material goods, food, or drink may be bound but still lives on. The Desert Fathers and Mothers came to realize that the struggle with these distorted desires is itself a gift. Through this struggle, we realize in intimate, personal terms that we cannot save ourselves. The power and the initiative always come from God. It is the grace of God that saves, not our willpower. But, if we want to know and feel the grace of God, we are not released from the never-ending struggle.

These first two Benedictine steps are about focusing our awareness on God and developing some detachment from the devices and desires of our hearts. They describe the interior habits of our hearts. In the next chapter we'll go a little deeper, exploring two steps that can only be followed once we have planted ourselves in a Christian community.

CHAPTER 3

Foundational Habits: Two Communal Steps

3. Practicing Sacred Obedience
4. Cultivating Patience

The process of restoring Leonardo's painting, *The Last Supper,* took over two decades. In part, the restoration took so long because it was a large painting in terrible condition—but there were additional impediments. Barcilon's request to have the room closed to the public was denied, and so she and the other restorers were constantly working with the noise and distractions of tourists. Worse, several different Italian bureaucracies had authority over various aspects of the work, any of which could stop the work to question and criticize. Finally, there was an ebb and flow to the availability of money to pay for the work, depending on the whims of governments, corporations, and individuals. Restoration required patiently working with others.

The painting's public restoration models an important lesson: just as Barcilon and the team had to work among the crowds and visitors, the task of restoring our souls to the image and likeness of God must occur in community. An eleventh-century French abbott, Bernard of Clairvaux, in his great commentary on the Twelve Steps of Humility, allows that we might make some progress on the first two steps of humility, which I have called keeping watch and desiring God above all, outside of a monastery. For steps three to twelve, however, Bernard insists that no progress is possible without being planted in a God-centered community.[16] If we are to know who we truly are, if we are to be stripped of those things that block us from love, and if we are to claim quiet self-mastery, we must be part of a community and stay put, at least for a long season. Stability is the key to this chapter's communal steps of practicing sacred obedience and cultivating patience. We plant ourselves in a Christian community and gradually allow ourselves to be deeply shaped by the story that community tells and the life that it lives.

Step Three:
Practicing Sacred Obedience

obedience for the love of God
— The Rule of Saint Benedict, 7:34

Benedict's third step emphasizes strict obedience to a superior. Like "humility," the word "obedience" has a well-earned negative reputation. If someone were to ask what word we associate with the word "obedience," we would probably say "blind." It's all too easy to conjure up the violent obedience of goose-stepping Nazis or the self-destructive obedience of the Kool-Aid drinkers of Jonestown.

Closer to home, if we ever took an introductory course in psychology, we probably learned about the Milgram experiments. These experiments placed Yale University undergraduates in a situation where they believed they were applying electrical shocks to people. They were not. The supposed victims were only actors. Other actors, dressed in lab coats, ordered the students to apply what the students believed to be steadily higher levels of electrical shocks, based on a dial. The majority of these Ivy Leaguers, on the orders of the people in lab coats, willingly administered shocks far in excess of any acceptable level of pain. The experiment is a reminder that we all have the potential to obey authority in a way that leads us to harm others and even ourselves.

Perhaps we wonder if obedience can be a virtue at all. Maybe we believe that wisdom is found instead in a stance of skepticism and self-reliance. Maybe our best stance is simply and always to question authority. Perhaps we are more likely to do good if we listen only to our own devices and desires. I suspect that all of us, at some level, have deep sympathy with the New Hampshire state motto, "Live Free or Die." If obedience is going to be a helpful word for us, it will probably require some serious rehabilitation.

Yet obedience does have another side. Just as it can be helpful to remember that the word humility shares a Latin root with the word for earth, *humus*, and so means not just groveling shame but groundedness, so it can be helpful to know that obedience shares a Latin root with the word to listen, *audare*. The obedient are those who listen well.

I love to sing and take great pleasure when I am able to be part of a chorus of voices that strikes a chord that rings clearly and powerfully. My small voice, in that moment, becomes a part of something exponentially larger than itself. Yet my voice has become something larger not by asserting itself but rather by listening and blending and submitting to the sound of the whole.

Listening did not come easily to me. In college I was a part of a men's *a cappella* singing group, essentially a traveling and performing fraternity. At the end of my first year in the group, I was given an award for being the least obedient, the one who did not listen. My ability to blend vocally was okay, but there was rarely a decision made or a project pursued that didn't include my voice chiming in with thoughts, opinions, and questions, most of them unsolicited. But I stuck with it, or rather they stuck with me, and I eventually became the president and emcee of the group.

Foundational Habits: Two Communal Steps

Now, one of my great joys in life is reuniting with my friends in the Society of Orpheus and Bacchus to sing the songs that are so deeply a part of me I feel as though I could never forget them. When I join the other first tenors in the final blast of a chord of "John Henry," our signature song, I know I am home. Learning obedience in the SOBs, the nickname for the group, gave me one of life's greatest gifts: a community of lifelong friends.

I have been told that when monks travel to other monastic communities, they can tell the health of the community by the quality of its singing. It is not a requirement to be a great singer to be a monk, and so the quality of the singing voices is almost always mixed. But good, loving, and healthy communities learn over time to blend their voices within the range of quality. I have a favorite CD, now sadly out of circulation, of the evening offices sung by English Carthusian monks. There aren't very many of the monks, and one is very old with a thin voice that often cracks. It doesn't matter. The brothers are united in their slow, attentive singing. The beauty is only enhanced by our ability, within the blend, to hear a few distinct, beloved voices.

Benedictine monks or nuns are rooted in just one community where they learn sacred obedience. The people with whom they sing are also the ones with whom they negotiate whose turn it is to do the dishes and where the money for the burst sewer pipe will come from. Our lives are likely to be more divided. Our household and our place of work are likely to be entirely separate from the place where we pray and explore the life of God with others. Eventually, we can learn to listen deeply to our spouses, parents, and children for the love of God. We can learn to obey our bosses, manage our employees, and deal with our clients as though each were Christ himself. We strive for whole, integrated lives. But to achieve that level of integration, we first need to be anchored in an intentional Christian community that teaches the ways of Jesus. There are three practices we can follow to begin learning this step of humility, even if we aren't monks or nuns. These practices are joining a Christian community, befriending the poor, and committing to a Discipleship Group.

Join a Christian Community

The first practice is to simply join—and stick with—a local Christian community. Even this can be hard. I have great sympathy for the bumper sticker that reads, "Jesus, save me from your followers!" There may be a part of all of us that wishes to cut to the chase and go straight to Jesus, without the mess of all of the rest of us who wish to be with him too. But that is not the way Jesus set things up. We see this as early as the first New Testament Christians, whom Paul persecuted. When the resurrected Jesus appeared to Paul on the road to Damascus, he asked Paul, "Why do you persecute *me*?" (Acts 9:4) As risky and strange as it may seem, Jesus chooses to associate himself so deeply with his community of followers that we are, mysteriously, his body. If you want to know Jesus, you are stuck with us.

Stability is the key. At the beginning of his *Rule*, Benedict divides monks into several different types. He reserves his greatest contempt for the type he calls *gyrovagues*, those who wander from one sacred community to another, never firmly planting themselves (THE RULE OF SAINT BENEDICT, 1:10-11). The name is evocative, conjuring a picture of someone who spins like a top or gyroscope and then never comes into sharp focus. Community life makes us clear and sharp. It slows us down, stops us spinning, and forces us to come into focus for others, with all the good and the bad we bring. We can fool some of the people some of the time, but if we stick around long enough, our whole selves will eventually come into view. If we are gyrovagues, we have the luxury of blaming each community we visit for its imperfections, never ourselves. The true image of a gyrovague is never revealed because their restoration work always gets stalled.

There is no perfect Christian community. Every church will eventually disappoint us. All communities have the same fatal flaw, which is that they are filled with people. Eventually any honeymoon experience ends, and then the real work begins. If we want to be part of a community, we first make a decision to show up consistently. The way we express this consistency in Discipleship Groups is the vow that says, "By God's grace, I will praise God, offering myself and receiving God's love and blessings with the rest of my Christian community in weekly 'worship... in the beauty of holiness'" (Psalm 96:9). Further, we have to trust that God has planted us in a particular church community for a reason and then stick with it until we discern very clear signs that it is time to leave. A helpful guideline is to think in terms of seven-year commitments. I was taught by my mentors—and my experience has confirmed—that seven years is often long enough to live through our mistakes and experience the fruit of our good works.

Within the Christian community, some of the most valuable people are those who have been through many of these seven-year cycles and so have inside them the lore and the experience of generations. If they have stayed spiritually alive, they become what in monastic circles are called Living Rules. The foundation of a healthy community resides in these Living Rules, these saints of sacred obedience.

I often think of Ann Hanson, who was one of the Living Rules of my own church. Ann was quiet, devout, and hardworking. Any healthy church has at least a handful of Anns who make the place run and give it its particular texture. At a certain point, Ann began to forget things. Tests eventually showed that the forgetfulness indicated a deeper illness. She was a widow without children, and so it fell to our community to care for her throughout the course of what turned out to be her last illness. In her final months, she received an outpouring of affection as we brought her meals, fixed her house, helped get her financial affairs in order, and arranged for appropriate hospice care.

One Sunday morning, as I was preparing to enter worship, I received the call that Ann had died. After services, about twenty of us went to her house and surrounded the bed where her body lay in her bedroom. In the early afternoon light, we said prayers for a vigil and then fell into silence. After a time, our head usher broke the silence by observing that there were now at least twenty of us who were going to try to fill Ann's shoes. We all laughed in recognition of a beautiful truth. Her spirit was so large that it had profoundly shaped our entire community. Each of us now had the task of continuing her faithful labor and, like her, we could do it with love and joy. Through sacred obedience, practiced through the course of a life, we too can become vessels through whom the goodness of God is passed from one generation to the next.

Befriend the Poor

The second practice is to become friends with the poor and the marginalized in the local community. *The Rule of Saint Benedict* states that "great care and concern are to be shown in receiving poor people and pilgrims, because in them particularly Christ is received" (THE RULE OF SAINT BENEDICT, 53:15). Hospitality for those on the margins ought to be a part of any Christian community. The churches are called to move outside the church walls to seek and serve those whom Jesus especially loves.

In the Discipleship Group vow, we promise to "endeavor to serve others everywhere I can, working toward giving an hour a week in service of the poor, remembering that Jesus said, "just as you did it to one of the least of these… you did it to me" (Matthew 25:40). Jesus is very clear that he means specific actions of clothing the naked, feeding the hungry, and visiting the sick and those in prison (Matthew 25:31-46). It does not include writing checks and serving on boards, as important as those actions may also be. To learn about sacred obedience, we must be face to face with the poor and, by grace, to be friends.

Finding a place to serve and befriend the poor may be as simple as volunteering at a local soup kitchen, but taking time to find a better fit can pay off. Some years ago, I spent several months with a parishioner, Beverly, going around to the various service agencies in our county for informational interviews. We wanted to find out what the needs were and discover where a community of our size might make a difference.

Eventually, we discovered a small school for probationary youth. This school is the last step before juvenile detention. At first, we organized a few after-school activities. Once the principal discovered we were trustworthy and serious, she asked us if we would tackle one of her greatest challenges: the health and readiness of the students. Attendance and performance at the school were low, and one of the many reasons for this was that the students showed up hungry. So six years ago, my church started serving hot breakfast several times a week to the youth. We call it the Teen Success Breakfast. Their attendance and performance have increased. By asking questions, listening, and showing up faithfully, we were able to make a difference. Sacred obedience bore fruit in the world.

For the volunteers at our Teen Success Breakfast, listening to the students can be painful. Their language is violent and filled with creative curses and stories of drug abuse. It is as though the volunteers are listening to the teens as they destroy themselves. Yet the students are just as often polite, respectful, and grateful so that the work of serving up made-to-order pancakes can inspire and lead to good-humored connection. The volunteers, the teachers, and the students have told me that the simple act of sharing hot breakfast has taught them about love.

If we dare to go beyond our comfort zone and do as Christ teaches, we are likely to experience reverse mission, particularly as our relationship grows toward genuine friendship.[17] We may initially believe we are bringing the

Foundational Habits: Two Communal Steps

compassion of Christ to the poor, that we are the ones going out in mission. But we often discover that the poor will teach us the way of Christ and so become missionaries to us if we only learn to listen.

One of the heaviest burdens many of us bear is that of casting judgment. The tradition of Saint Benedict, going back to the Desert Fathers, offers stern warnings against the temptation of judging the acts of others. Here's one example among many:

> Abbot John used to say: We have thrown down a light
> burden, which is the reprehending of our own selves,
> and we have chosen the heavy burden, by justifying
> our own selves and condemning others.[18]

There are probably many people in our lives we secretly condemn. The poor are often at the top of this list of contempt. The best and perhaps only way to remove this toxin from our lives is to be with the poor often enough that we finally see clearly our shared human dignity. Face to face relations give restoration.

Starting in my twenties, I felt drawn to be with and serve homeless teens. Growing up I had read many stories about the intertwined depravity and glamour of heroin, particularly with rock stars and jazz musicians. Being with homeless teens, many of whom were addicts, helped me release these preconceptions. Kurt was a young man about my age with dilated eyes and a chipped front tooth. From my conversations with him at a drop-in center in Seattle, I felt the gentle, doomed sadness of the addiction. He was not some other creature but a deeply sympathetic human being.

Later, when I moved to California, I met Stephen who told me that taking heroin was like getting a whole body hug.

What kind of life must you have had to need to search for hugs in an addiction that slowly kills both mind and body? I have not been purged of either the judgment against addiction or the sense of its glamour. Both are far too insidious and deeply woven in me for that. But now, judgment and glamour are most often outweighed by a sense of sweetness for our common need for hugs and sadness at our failure to hug. Deep listening to these poor, homeless, addicted teens has slowly given me at least a small taste of Jesus' compassion and forgiveness.

Commit to a Discipleship Group

In most dating relationships there comes a time when a profound question must be answered. "Is this the person with whom I want to spend the rest of my life?" The next steps in the relationship will be deeply affected by our hopes, or lack of them, for a long-term future. Discipleship Groups encapsulate so much of the spiritual dynamic of The Restoration Project that something similar is at stake. If this feels like the path God would have you follow in order to have a deeper loving relationship with God, neighbor, and self, then committing yourself to a Discipleship Group is, in all likelihood, the best next step for you.

Discipleship Groups are part of a strong Christian tradition of small groups. Jesus began the church by drawing to himself a small group of apostles whom he challenged and loved into becoming leaders. In America, among the first churches to rediscover the power of small groups was the Church of the Saviour in Washington, D.C. This ecumenical church founded by Gordon and Mary Cosby inspired much of The Restoration Project. One of Cosby's early discoveries was that unless you deliberately structured your small group to be about mission and spiritual growth, it would always end up as a self-support group. Of course, for any Christian group to be authentic, it must have the capacity to offer care and support. However, unless structures intentionally create means to encourage growth and outreach, the important elements will not happen.

Discipleship Groups are generally composed of five to nine people who meet either every week or every other week for at least an hour. What distinguishes Discipleship Groups from other Christian small groups is the liturgy that begins and ends every meeting. Each gathering begins with a time of silence and a statement of intention read by the leader. Then there are six vows that are read aloud, each in turn by a different member of the group. A seventh, final, vow is read by all. These vows make an explicit commitment to work toward lives with regular prayer, worship, service, generosity, learning, discerning of call, and commitment to the Discipleship Group. The entire liturgy can be found in the back of this book.

These seven vows emerged gradually, as a range of Discipleship Groups came into being across the country. Together, we were striving to find a limited set of vows that would express a genuine desire to follow the teachings of Jesus. Each of the vows as we now have them are expressed gently. In each, we say we are working toward the desired rhythm or goal, whether it is twenty minutes a day of prayer, giving away ten percent of our income, or learning all of the Bible. I do not believe anyone, including me, joined a Discipleship Group already fulfilling the expectations of all seven vows.

The point of the vows is to encourage us to grow into the regular practice of classic Christian disciplines.

Three elements of Discipleship Groups are particularly helpful when it comes to nurturing the virtue of sacred obedience. These are commitment, confidentiality, and sense of call.

Obedience begins with commitment. Most days, in my morning prayer, there are a limited number of people I can focus on with individual attention. I always pray for my wife and two boys, and I have developed the habit of thinking about the people I am likely to encounter that day and praying for them. For the last two years, part of my commitment is also to regularly pray for Vladimir, Jerry, John, and Jacob, the members of my Discipleship Group. It is a simple act. I say their names in my mind and then let my general impressions and thoughts emerge. I remember what they told me about their lives in our group meetings, and if they asked for prayer for anything, I do it.

It may not seem like much, but the very act of carrying around someone else in our hearts is a fundamental Christian act. It signifies that we are not concerned solely with ourselves, but understand that by our baptism we have been adopted into a much larger, more diverse family than we could ever have conceived or created by ourselves. By committing to a Discipleship Group, we are turning the abstract commitments of baptism into reality. Jerry, John, Jacob, and Vladimir are my brothers in Christ because I carry them in my heart and they carry me in theirs. We are bound to each other.

This commitment is expressed in the final vow of the Discipleship Group's opening liturgy: "By God's grace, we have joined ourselves to one another as this Discipleship

Group, and we commit to meeting regularly for this season of our lives, believing that 'if we love one another, God lives in us, and his love is perfected in us' (I John 4:12)."

I sometimes go to our weekly meetings reluctantly. Maybe I feel tired or would simply prefer to stay home with my family eating dinner. But I never leave with regrets. After the opening liturgy, we almost always spend time checking in with each other. For that period of just under an hour, I am sharply attuned to the reality of these people's lives. Through a slow accumulation of stories and details, I have gotten some insight into their struggles and successes, into their dreams and disappointments. Obedience is the practice of listening well to my friends, without judgment or feeling that I need to solve a problem or inspire a solution. Likewise, their careful and good-humored listening to me inspires me to be honest and even daring in what I confess and tell. Commitment breeds good listening.

The second essential feature is confidentiality. At both the beginning and the end of each Discipleship Group meeting, there is a reminder that these converations are to be held in confidence. The value of a small group is completely dependent on how honest and vulnerable we are willing to be. If we show up every week anxious and protective, we are unlikely to get at the truth of who we are, what God intends for us, and how others can help us get there. In our groups, we are gradually invited, as we build trust, to lay aside all the masks and other protective habits and be our whole real selves. One of my favorite emails of all time was one sent to a listserv I ran when I served in Los Angeles as the leader of a Christian 20s/30s group. A longtime member, out of the blue, posted a note where he thanked us for letting him be his "weird self." Like so many in that group, and indeed like so many of us around the country, he spent a lot of time trying to fool people into thinking he was better, more charming, more intelligent, more everything than he actually was or felt. At least in one Christian group, this man felt he could set all that aside and just be himself, including his wonderful, charming, and engaging weirdness.

Discipleship Groups should be places of great safety and invitation. They should be places where we can admit the depth of our fears and anxieties. They should be places where we can finally speak aloud that great, wild, daring dream we have had since childhood. They should even be places where the occasional tacky, poorly conceived rage attack can come and go without permanent damage. The truth will set us free. But most of us need to know we are safe on our way to embracing the truth. Confidentiality is one of the key elements in the safety—and the genuine listening—of a small group.

The final key to nurturing the virtue of sacred obedience in the Discipleship Group is an ongoing focus on call. The sixth vow is "By God's grace, I will listen for God's call on my life, confident that I have been given 'a manifestation of the Spirit for the common good' (1 Corinthians 12:7), entrusting my Discipleship Group to test and support that call." Each of us has a unique piece of work in the world we are invited to complete in each era of our lives. The joy and challenge of being Christian is listening for that work and doing it. Following our call is one of the highest forms of Christian obedience. Discipleship Groups can be an essential component in discovering our unique call because, if we have been honest and vulnerable, it is a community of people who know us well. They are people who can speak the truth to us in love.

A call can take a variety of forms in relationship to a Discipleship Group. One mark of a call is that, through it, we serve others. And so at my church, I can see a direct connection between the depth and reliability of the Teen Success Breakfast and our Discipleship Groups. The backbone of our volunteer team is people in Discipleship Groups. These volunteers are not only reliable and cheerful, but they also are great storytellers. Their small groups give them the support and encouragement they need to follow their call to serve.

Calls can also be intensely personal. In my group, one member has a spouse with advanced cancer. Over the last year, we have supported him as he's gradually released other things from his life so he can focus on caring for her in every way possible. We have helped him keep up his sense of humor and reminded him that this is a season in his life and that other things will emerge. For myself, I was recently faced with a rather deep dilemma around how I was called to serve. My Discipleship Group was the one place in my church where I could be honest about my dilemma without causing needless anxiety or fear. I knew that from my brothers I would receive calm, patient, loving wisdom, and I did.

Receiving and following a call is more of an art than a science. Nonetheless, there are reliable guides that God is in the mix. Is the call persistent? Is it energizing? Is it shared—that is, do other recognize the call? Jacob and I are wrestling together with a sense of call. Last October we had a conversation with Diane, the executive director of the Ritter Center, one of the two major help organizations for the poor in San Rafael. St. Paul's has been a supporter of Ritter for decades. In the course of the conversation, we discovered that we were their major faith-based supporter, which came as some surprise. Also a surprise was what little support she feels from most faith communities here. Then, the director began to spell out for us her major vision.

Marin County, where San Rafael is located, has a chronic problem of homelessness. The most effective and proven way to address homelessness is through a system called permanent supportive housing. The problem though is that the community must first acknowledge that there's a homeless problem and then find the property to set up the housing. Both of these are profound challenges in Marin, which is terrible at facing its own pockets of brokenness and where Not In My Back Yard is a common rallying cry.

As the months have gone by, Jacob and I have repeatedly returned to our October conversation with Diane. When we have these conversations, we become animated and passionate. It does not seem right that the affluent county where we live can't face this basic human problem squarely. Further, we each have the sense that we may have a role to play in helping Diane's dream become a reality. Jacob works for a major non-profit in San Francisco and knows in great detail how permanent supportive housing works. I am well connected with the faith communities in Marin and feel confident that I can find others to help lead the invitation to Marin to do the right thing by embracing this kind of housing for the homeless. Our conversations are persistent, energizing, and shared. They may very well represent a call for both of us, if we will only obey.

Jesus has always had a lot of admirers, but that is not what he asks for. He wants followers. These groups are called

Discipleship Groups because in them we hold each other in his love and encourage each other to practice the disciplines he taught. These groups are a road-tested way to get off of the bleachers and on to the playing field, obeying our unique call.

Step Four:
Cultivating Patience

his heart quietly embraces suffering
— THE RULE OF SAINT BENEDICT, 7:35

Patience is the fourth step that creates the sure foundation of our own restoration project. Patience is the virtue that allows us to stay focused in the midst of the bustle of daily life; it also allows us to remain faithful to our deepest spiritual longings over the course of our lifetime. But it is no coincidence that Benedict places patience just after obedience. Patience is required when we are embracing community. Benedict well knows that it is no easy thing to listen attentively to the needs, desires, and commands of others, which so often run against our own impulses.

Cultivating Patience with Others

We learn patience, above all, by the people we know and love. We learn by watching and emulating people like Ann Hanson, the Living Rule of St. Paul's congregation for many years. We learn by simply staying faithful to our friends, family members, and fellow parishioners even when they seem tiresome or difficult. One close friend and parishioner had the courage to be honest with me about his relationship with a member of our community who is poor, struggles with mental illness, and can be persistent and disruptive. My friend

Foundational Habits: Two Communal Steps

said, "To be honest, I can't stand him, but I'm afraid he may be Jesus!" The poor man is teaching my close friend patience.

The first time I read *The Rule of Saint Benedict* the detail that struck me the most was how severely and often Benedict attacked the sin of grumbling. There are many human faults revealed in community. Why single out that one?

As I have devoted my life to nurturing healthy, thriving Christian communities, I have come to see the wisdom of Benedict's admonitions against grumbling, against those casually disparaging remarks about each other or about our common life. Of course more cruel and profound ways to undermine each other exist. But it is precisely because grumbling can seem so innocuous that it needs to be cut off. We are all tempted to grumble and complain from time to time. Worse, we are in the habit of having our grumbling make it clear that whatever is wrong is clearly not our fault. Our grumbling is a subtle way of marking out our own superiority and, perhaps, our own paradoxically powerful status as a pitiable victim. Grumbling is a subtle and persistent path to self-glorification and community denigration.

Patience is the virtue that releases the habit of grumbling. I previously referred to the ancient Christian practice now called centering prayer. The practice is to sit still in a comfortable position for at least twenty minutes with your eyes closed. When thoughts come to your mind, release them ever so gently. The technique is to pick a one-syllable word like "love" or "faith" and then use that word to gently encourage the thought to move along. No matter how holy or profound the thought seems to be in the moment, we are to let it go, trusting that the truly important will come back around when needed. The goal of the time of prayer is simply to make oneself as open and responsive to God's presence and initiative as possible.

When we are in community with other people, countless opportunities to grumble will present themselves. There will be people who, in our view, talk too much, or don't do enough to help, or seem manipulative or cruel. In a fit of generosity, we might take on some hard piece of work, only to find no one has noticed. Our temptation will be to draw attention and sympathy with our grumbling. In that moment of temptation, patience consists in the internal practice of acknowledging the thought and then letting it go, like a thought in centering prayer, before it crosses our lips.

Churches should always be two things simultaneously: schools for saints and hospitals for sinners. On the good side, they ought to be schools, helping to draw out of us our best, teaching us the skills and practices that help us, in imitation of our Lord, to be humble, loving, and wise. At the same time, in an acknowledgement of the broken place where each of us starts, it ought to be a hospital. There is much sickness in us that needs to be healed on our way to sanctity, and it will take time. In any church, we are always going to be surrounded with other recovering sinners like ourselves. Among the great gifts we can give each other is to release the temptation to grumble at each other's brokenness.

Discipleship Groups provide an intensification of this process of Christian community building through which, in our tradition, we are saved. The people in an honest, mature group will give us more to grumble about, not less! This is because, over time, we will come to know the full glory and shame of each person in our group, and none of us is perfect. Far from it. We each bring into any group our own mixture of good gifts and bad impulses. Part of the purpose of a group is to help us face our negative impulses squarely and to work through them. Experiencing such a process, both in ourselves and in others, requires patience.

A guideline in the formation of any kind of small-group ministry is the rule of thirds. One third of small groups will fall apart, one third will stumble along, and one third will thrive. I have found this guideline stays true for Discipleship Groups. This means that, once again, patience will likely be required on our way to building intimacy and trust in order to spiritually thrive.

For members of The Restoration Project, thriving means hearing God's call on our lives and following it. In a mixture of metaphor, this process of hearing and following call is often called "discernment." To discern something means to see the rough outline of a thing and then, through careful and persistent looking, have the details of the object slowly come into view. Those who have actively pursued the knowledge of God's call have frequently found that the process of call is similar. We may have a vague sense of what we ought to be doing in the world, but it is only through time, persistence, and care that we can slowly become clear and confident in what we are meant to do and then build the confidence and support to pursue it. We can't type "my call from God" into Google and expect a reliable response. Helping others discern call requires patience with others just as surely as discerning our own call requires patience with ourselves.

Cultivating Patience with Ourselves

The importance of this fourth step of patience is reflected in how long Benedict takes to describe it. While he dispatches with some of the steps in only a sentence, this single step takes up eight sentences in its English translation. The most important phrase in this long step is Benedict's description of the interior state of one who is learning patience. He writes that the "heart quietly embraces suffering" (THE RULE OF SAINT BENEDICT, 7:35). The metaphor of a quiet embrace suggests that our hearts face life with a stance that is a middle place between cowering fear and angry aggression. A heart that is capable of quietly embracing suffering is a heart with great poise and equanimity. There are two practices I have found helpful in gradually nurturing an interior attitude of patience. Both have helped my heart quietly embrace suffering and so to become more patient. One is remembering an image of some American heroes and the other is embracing scripture's power to gradually shape my spiritual imagination.

I carry around in my mind a mental picture that has grown from my admiration of those who led the Civil Rights Movement. I particularly think of what they learned about non-violent protest. The pioneers of this practice in India initially thought it would be best to lay down in a fetal position when attacked. They discovered that laying down always escalated the violence. Protesters were kicked even harder. As they reflected and learned, protesters learned to stay standing and maintain non-threatening eye contact with the police or other hostile forces.[19] When life becomes frustrating and difficult, I hold on to this image of the strong middle way. The challenges I face are to be neither blindly attacked nor are they to be fearfully submitted to. Instead, I imagine that I can stand firm, with dignity and with clear vision. I imagine that those non-violent Civil Rights protesters were models to us of Christian patience.

Our hearts are not only trained by images. They are also trained by stories, and the most important story is the one told by the whole of the Bible. As a reminder, a devotion to scripture is one of the seven vows of Discipleship Groups: "By God's grace, I will 'read, mark, learn and inwardly digest the Holy Scriptures, trusting that they are inspired by God' for my 'training in righteousness,' working toward knowledge of the entire book" (2 Timothy 3:16).

A deeper and broader knowledge of the Bible can lead us to at least two scriptural insights that are particularly helpful in training our hearts to quietly embrace suffering. The first is a deep understanding of the cross. The cross is the ultimate expression of the consistent scriptural theme of the suffering servant. The Bible teaches that the full expression of love in this fallen world always seems to have a cost. Moses suffered the complaints of the people and, in the end, did not enter the Promised Land. Job lost everything before ultimately being restored to great prosperity. The servant in Isaiah is spat upon and rejected as the necessary experience to heal his people's wounds. Jesus continues this pattern and tells us we must do the same. He bids us to pick up our cross daily as we follow him.

The pattern of the suffering servant continues in the most influential stories in our popular culture. Frodo, Gandalf, and Aragorn each go through near-death experiences on their path to triumph over evil in *The Lord of the Rings* series. Aslan suffers death and the Pevensies suffer betrayal before the White Witch is conquered and spring returns to Narnia in *The Lion, the Witch, and the Wardrobe.* Harry Potter is an essentially homeless orphan who must lose his new mentor, Dumbledore, and his new home, Hogwarts, in his triumph over Voldemort and the Death Eaters.

Each of these stories deliberately echoes the definitive story of Jesus. They derive their power from the fundamental truth of Jesus' story of life-giving suffering. When we know the whole of the scriptural story by heart, we too are capable of writing grand stories of suffering patiently endured on the way to greater life and love. There will be anguish and pain on our way toward the peace that passes all understanding. Jesus' story of death and resurrection helps us reframe our trials so that our hearts can quietly embrace suffering with the faith that death is not the end and that love conquers all.

The second helpful insight that can train our hearts in patience is to allow scripture to shift our perception of time. There are two Greek words in the New Testament that we translate as "time." One is *chronos,* and it is the source of our English word "chronology." It means time like we tell it on a clock. Chronos time is passing steadily and inexorably. There is a date on the calendar when we were born, and there will be a date on the calendar, still unknown, when we will die. Time marches on.

The other Greek word for time is *kairos.* It is the word Jesus uses in his most concise mission statement, which occurs at the beginning of the gospel of Mark. There he declares "the time [kairos] is fulfilled, and the kingdom of God has come near, repent, and believe in the good news" (Mark 1:15). Reading the whole of scripture invites us to know and experience the fulfillment of time with little tastes of this heavenly *kairos*.

I know of one surefire way to experience *kairos* with the help of scripture and in the context of community. About fifteen years ago in a monastery library, I stumbled across a tourist pamphlet from Little Gidding. This house was the home of a brief experiment in Christian living in England in the seventeenth century. Families lived together and kept a kind of monastic rule centered on worship from *The Book of Common Prayer*. They were well regarded by many and even played host to King Charles I three times. Their leader, Nicholas Ferrar, was a close friend and confidant of Anglican priest and poet George Herbert. Centuries later, T.S. Eliot would name one of his *Four Quartets* after the house.

I read in the pamphlet that one of the practices of Little Gidding was to gather as a community and to say the entire Psalter in one sitting. I was intrigued and wanted to give it a try. Upon returning to my seminary, I reserved the prayer chapel and with the help of some friends, dove right in. I have since read the Psalter aloud with friends in its entirety six separate times with three different communities. When I do it, people are invited to come and go as they please. Each time, I am joined by somewhere in the range of ten to thirty people, and there have always been a small handful who make it all the way through. We go in a circle with each person deciding how the next psalm will be said or sung. We continue until we are finished, usually with one short break for a light dinner.

The experience takes about five hours, but it is a most peculiar five hours. I cannot tell you whether the time passes slowly or flies by. It does neither. Time shifts, somehow, into a kind of deep stillness. There is always a kind of thickness that comes into the air that makes the present seem so present that our shared sense of time is changed. By the end, I feel as though I have been on a retreat many days long. Despite being relatively sedentary for five hours, I am not restless. With my brothers and sisters in Christ, I have been in the kind of time that Jesus promises, a time fulfilled. It is *kairos* time to me. My heart is strong and at rest. The words of the psalms, which encompass all possible human experience before God, have given us the strength to quietly and with great compassion and forgiveness embrace our allotment of human suffering.[20]

Foundational Habits: Two Communal Steps

CHAPTER 4

The Image of God

5. Seeing the Image of God in Ourselves

Barcilon and her team were prudent in how they restored *The Last Supper.* They knew that for most of the twentieth century, those responsible for the care of the painting deliberately left the unwanted gunk. They were afraid that if they started cleaning too vigorously they would strip away the work of Leonardo along with the pollution and the crude repainting. After careful study and scientific advances—and thanks to good taste, Barcilon's team reached a point where they were ready to strip the painting of all that was not from the master.

The greatest help for Barcilon and her team for understanding what Leonardo intended for the faces was a series of Leonardo's drawings now at Windsor Castle. Some are mere sketches, where a beautifully drawn line indicates a precise expression of the mouth. Others, for example Simon's head, are careful studies that reproduce the way skin folds together at the back of the craning neck of an old man.[21] The sketches of the master showed them the true intentions of his painting.

Where can we look to find reliable sketches of our true selves, made in the image of God? As Christians, we are always called to look first to the words and images of scripture. But we have also been blessed with holy women and men who, through the centuries, have proven to be reliable guides to learning about God and ourselves. The portrayals of human experience they have left us are still useful and dependable. We have been looking at the art of one of those holy people, Saint Benedict. In this chapter, I invite you to think and pray alongside one of the people who inspired him, Saint Augustine.

The Image of God

Step Five:
Seeing the Image of God
in Ourselves

a person does not conceal

— THE RULE OF SAINT BENEDICT, 7:44

In *The Rule of Saint Benedict*, the fifth step is "that a man does not conceal from his abbot any sinful thoughts entering his heart, or any wrongs committed in secret but rather confesses them humbly. Concerning this, scripture exhorts us: Make known your way to the Lord and hope in him." (THE RULE OF SAINT BENEDICT, 7:44-5) In order to become mature we must cultivate the skill of speaking honestly about ourselves without illusion or evasion. Because we were made in the image of God and yet reveal to the world something far less, the truth about ourselves is some ugliness layered over great beauty. Part of our work of restoration is being able to see the beauty underneath the grime.

I invite us to claim the greatest beauty in ourselves by exploring three areas of our lives in depth and learning to speak adeptly about them. In each of these areas, it will be like we are spelunking, going down into the depths of our human experience. Because we are made in the image of God, we are each unfathomably deep mysteries. But the fact that the cave has no bottom doesn't mean we can't take our flashlights and try to go down to some depth in each of these areas.

In these reflections I am imitating Saint Augustine. In his book, *On the Trinity*, he invites those who seek after God to take with total seriousness the biblical claim that we are made in God's image. Furthermore, he starts with our core belief that God is both one and three, traditionally named Father, Son and Holy Spirit. If we were made in the image of God, then we too must somehow be both one and three.

Through the course of the book, Augustine finds and tests a series of trinities within the human person. These include mind, knowledge, and love; sight, seeing, and the thing seen; and memory, understanding, and will. In each case, Augustine finds things that are similar to the Trinity—and things that don't match so well. But he always proceeds with great confidence that somewhere within our human capacities is the image of the Trinity and that even the search itself will yield insight.[22] He never arrives at one perfect analogy, and suggests that others might continue to explore this mystery of a trinity in our human souls.

Inspired by Augustine, I want to offer a trinity of our human capacities as a way of thinking about God's image in us. This trinity is our capacities to remember, to receive, and to love. I invite you to think and remember and explore with me. What is in our memory and which memories do we choose to dwell on? Whom do we receive into our hearts and how do we treat them? Whom do we love, and how? By exploring our own memory, hospitality, and love, I wonder if we might, by grace, see at least a rough sketch of God's image in ourselves.

Remembering God

When my wife Chloe was in college, her mother, Claire, developed terminal cancer. When she was very close to death, Chloe's father Lyman called all the family to come to her bedside in California and keep vigil. Chloe and I had been dating for about a year, and I had gotten to know her whole family. I waited back in Connecticut and talked with Chloe every day to hear how things were unfolding.

As Claire was lying in the hospital bed, immobilized in the last days of her life, one of the things Lyman did was to take her hand and lead her through a common memory. They had spent some of the best years of their lives in a house near a medieval village in the south of France. Every morning Claire would take a brisk walk to the village, passing some small farms and a convent that had been converted into a private estate. She would walk up the narrow streets and alleys of the village to the church at the top of the village where she would stretch in the churchyard as she looked out over the valley. She would then descend to the bakery to buy baguettes and croissants for her family. As Lyman held Claire's hand, he described, in great loving detail, each stage of her morning walk: the mottled horse in the field of the farm, the light as it began to hit the medieval stone, the fountain underneath the ancient archway.

Our memories are among our most powerful human capacities. They give our life its sense of meaning and fullness, and define and even redeem our most significant relationships. Saint Augustine called memory "fields and spacious palaces where lie the treasures of innumerable images of all kinds of things brought into it by the senses."[23] For all of us, the contents of our "fields and spacious palaces" are a decidedly mixed bag. The lyrics from 1970s disco tunes lie side by side with snippets of scripture. Memories of high school athletic triumphs are next to memories of high school sexual shame. Recollections of a fabulous dinner party are close to memories of the wedding to which we were not invited.

Part of the work of radical self-knowledge is to carefully tend the wild, lush, and sometimes unruly fields of our memories. A good place to begin is by calling to mind moments that seemed particularly graceful. That is, we can heed Paul's advice in Philippians: "Whatever is true, whatever is honorable, whatever is just, whatever is pure, whatever is pleasing, whatever is commendable, if there is any excellence and if there is anything worthy of praise, think about these things" (Philippians 4:8). Among the greatest of "these things" are the experiences of our lives where we felt closest to God.

Most of us never speak of these experiences and rarely bring them to mind. A practice for recovering the image of God in us is to dare to remember and celebrate the moments in our lives when we felt intimacy with God. Perhaps we can try to do this ourselves by taking some time to write out brief accounts, or even just a list, of three memories. Even better, we can seek a small community like a Discipleship Group where we can tell our stories and hear the stories of others.

At the heart of the spiritual life of my church is an experience I call Basic Discipleship. A group of four to six of us meets for five or six weeks to encourage each other in a rhythm of daily prayer and to share our stories. In the first session, I always tell three stories from my own life. For example, I might recount the time, back when I thought I was an atheist, when I was recruited at the last minute to assist at a worship service. As the service began, I found I couldn't contain my tears as I saw and felt the packed church in hushed anticipation, awaiting the presence of God. Or I might relate the time I was sitting in silent meditation and the presence of God burst inside my heart like a fountain of water, cleansing and strengthening me, turning me from a seeker of God to a believer in Jesus. And I might tell of the time I was simply standing at the end of a dock on a pond and, as I looked, the nature around me seemed to throb with the presence of life, of God.

Each week in our group, a different person tells his or her story. I've found that everyone has stories, some subtle and others dramatic. Some stories are about church, some about friendship, others about nature, and still others are about experiences of sickness and death. Always, there are people in a small Basic Discipleship class who have never told these stories in their lives. The stories are the treasure hidden in the often untended garden of their memories. Many times, our experiences of God are peculiar and even hard to fit into our usual categories of what is "real." Sometimes we may be almost ashamed of them. One beauty of an experience like Basic Discipleship is that hearing other people's stories so often evokes or helps us recover memories of our own, memories that may be buried. Our work is to recover and claim the experiences God has already given us.

Another practice is to "read, mark, learn and inwardly digest"[24] the scriptures and other reliable Christian spiritual writings. Our goal is to fill our memories with the words and images that are most likely to lead us to the image of God, and we do this best by a daily practice of prayer. Our minds are filled with detritus and data. I can recall once coming back to Los Angeles from an evening spent at a hilltop monastery in Santa Barbara. For about half the drive back on Highway 101, the ocean was to my right and hills to the left. My mind was free to wander or to simply gaze at and appreciate the scenery before me. As I passed through Ventura and approached Los Angeles, however, I saw my first billboard, and it was a fairly explicit one of a woman and a beer. The marketers had done a professional job of plugging into the primal part of my brain and so, for several miles, my mind and memory were filled with women and beer. Unwittingly, if only briefly, my memory and imagination had been shaped.

The other part of the experience of Basic Discipleship is getting into the rhythm of twenty minutes of prayer a day, anchored in scripture. Like any other practice, there will be dry patches where it seems like nothing is happening. However, we will experience an effect over time. We will be driving in our car, with the radio turned off, no sexy billboards in sight, and a phrase from scripture—perhaps "the peace of God, which surpasses all understanding" (Phillippians 4:7) or "your faith has saved you; go in peace" (Luke 7:50) or simply "Abide in me" (John 15:4) —will gently come into our mind and envelop our being, filling us with the curious warmth of gratitude and presence. A daily practice of prayer gradually fills our memories with words, images, thoughts, and feelings that can, at any moment of the day, draw us closer to God. We lead very distracted lives with each day offering more stimulation than our poor brains can handle. Twenty minutes focused solely on our relationship with God provides an essential spiritual balance to the worldly weight of each day.

The Image of God

We can connect even deeper with God through our capacity of memory, but in order to glimpse this truth we need to go beyond our usual understanding of memory. Imagine that within our spacious palace of memory, there is a secret, hidden room in the basement foundation. Although this room is in everyone's mansion, not all venture down into the dark to seek it. The room is locked much of the time, and, because the keys to unlocking the room make no sense, there are even fewer who unlock it and enter. And even those who enter only ever stay a brief time before they are called back to the upper floors. In this basement room are kept the primal stories that tell us who we are, where we came from, and where we are going. Often, to hear them as they are meant to be heard, we must listen again as a little child.

Here is one example. We are all sons and daughters of Adam and Eve. Once upon a time Adam and Eve dwelt in a place that was perfect, their every need easily attended to in perfect proportion. They looked around at creation and everything they saw showed the masterful hand of God, their creator. Above all, they never, not even for one instant, doubted that they were loved by God or by each other. Adam and Eve rested in perfect knowledge of love. Then, tragically, they made a bad choice. It is a mystery why they did it. Mere curiosity? Why, when God had asked of them only one thing, did they go against the request?

But they did it, and in that moment something snapped, something broke, and paradise receded from view. Those of us who are sons of Adam and daughters of Eve have deep in our consciousness, in the palace of our minds, memories of paradise, and hints of the tragic moment when paradise was lost. We carry them with us like a phantom limb or the space in our mouth from a missing tooth. Part of cultivating our memories to recover the image of God is opening ourselves to these stories that remind us of our ancient and true myth of creation, fall, and redemption.

Receiving Jesus

One of my favorite poets is a man named James Merrill. Before his death in the mid-1990s, many called him America's greatest living poet. His poems are elegant, precise, and deeply felt. They also reveal a person who seemed to me both generous and kind. My impression was confirmed when I went with my friend Candler to hear Merrill read his poetry. The large lecture hall was packed with an appreciative audience, but at the event's end, we were able to make our way up to the front to meet him. Candler's mother was a distant cousin of Merrill's, and he remembered brief visits from the poet when he was a child. As soon as Candler introduced himself, Merrill's eyes lit up. He couldn't have been more kind, attentive, or present. Years later, after he died, I found out that he was well-known for his ability to make and keep friends. When it came to friendship, it was said of him that his heart was like "wax to receive and marble to retain."[25] He was soft and receptive when meeting a new friend, and firm and loyal once the friendship was made.

Most of us aren't so gracious in either receiving or remaining faithful to our friends. Like our memories, our record of friendship is likely to be a mixed bag. Some friends we are faithful to. We return their emails promptly and take the initiative to call them. Perhaps we carry them in our hearts, wondering how they would react to certain situations.

The Image of God

We hear a new piece of music and think they might like it. We wonder from time to time how their marriage is going.

Other friends we let slip away. We hesitate to return calls. When we do think of them, we realize it's the first time we have remembered them in months.

In John's Gospel, Jesus says, "I do not call you servants... but I have called you friends" (John 15:15). Most Sundays, we have the opportunity to play host to the greatest guest and friend, Jesus. How we receive and hold him in those moments and in the time afterward is the center of how we discover and nurture the image of God. Jesus is present in many ways in a Sunday morning church experience. Examples include the words of the scripture, the work of the pastor in making a connection between the scripture and our daily lives, and the kindness and hospitality of the members of the community. But for me and for many others, there is nothing as reliable or as moving as the act of eating the bread and drinking the wine with our baptized brothers and sisters in Christ.

The church remembers that on the night before he died, Jesus took bread and wine, said "this is my body and blood," shared the food and drink with his friends, and told them to do the same in remembrance of him. He also said, in my favorite words in all of scripture, "abide in me as I abide in you." (John 15:4). Every Sunday, I feel like I am enacting Jesus' command to me by having him abide in me, in my body, through the primal acts of eating and drinking.

At my church, the communion bread is made by a parishioner. It is a special recipe that creates perfect small cakes that break easily so they can be shared. The bread has a distinctive, delicious taste. The recipe includes milk and honey as a very subtle reminder of the Old Testament promise that God would lead the people of Israel into a good land, a land of milk and honey. The bread is a reminder that Jesus is our way, as Christians, to the Promised Land.

The wine, too, is distinctive. It is ruby port, a thick, heavy wine. It's not the kind of wine you would have with a meal because it's too heavy. But for communion, just a sip feels rich and significant. When we leave the altar, we feel like we have been fed. Even ten and fifteen minutes later, we can still taste the communion meal.

But what happens then? Our bodies process the bread and wine like any other food and drink, but from the start we have been invited to imagine that something else is going on. We are asked to carry the presence of Jesus in our lives beyond the doors of the church and into our lives. Years ago I read a strange and wonderful image from a late nineteenth-century mystic, Richard Meux Benson. He had communion every day and imagined that with each Eucharistic meal a part of him was being replaced with part of Jesus. He believed our spiritual heart is like our skin. Several times a year our skin is shed and replaced with new material while still keeping its form. By receiving Jesus on a regular basis, we are restored to God's image and likeness, each piece of Christ's spiritual body replacing our own.[26]

Our task is to keep showing up, to keep saying yes to this presence of Jesus in our lives. Bread and wine are only outward and visible signs of an inward and invisible movement of God's love in our lives. The inward and invisible movement of love and grace and presence is not limited to communion or the preacher's pulpit. Jesus, at the end of the Gospel of Matthew, says, "and remember, I am with you always, to the end of the age" (Matthew 28:20). And I believe he meant it.

In ways known and, more often, unknown, Jesus is always with those who seek to know him.

For some, in some specially graced moments, Jesus appears in ways that are impossible to deny. From scripture we know that even after his death and even after all the appearances to his disciples after the resurrection, Jesus appeared to Paul on the road to Damascus. In one of the most moving contemporary stories of conversion, Anne Lamott tells how Jesus appeared to her as she hit rock bottom in her addiction to marijuana and alcohol. One night, after a binge, she feels that someone is in the room with her, and with a kind of deep knowing, she recognizes Jesus. She writes, "I felt him just sitting there on his haunches in the corner of my sleeping loft, watching me with patience and love, and I squinched my eyes shut, but that didn't help because that's not what I was seeing him with."[27]

I have a very sane friend who was serving in the military. One night as he was sleeping on the upper bed of a bunk bed, he woke up and Jesus was *right there*, standing by the bunk bed, his head and shoulders visible, holding his gaze. Soon after, my friend left the military to become a minister. And my friend isn't alone in this type of vision. A parishioner was once walking up the center of the chapel at a retreat center. He looked to the side, and there was Jesus walking beside him. What struck him was that Jesus was the exact same height as himself.

I have only had a few elusive experiences myself. One was on an eight-day retreat where I was encouraged to use my imagination. As a former amateur actor, it was delightful for me to follow the pattern of the Ignatian spiritual exercises under the daily guidance of a fine director. I found myself particularly drawn to the apostle Peter and spent time imagining what he was like and what it might have been like for him to traverse the ups and downs of his relationship with Jesus. Peter, after all, is the one who has the faith and insight to say to Jesus, "You are the Messiah" (Matthew 16:16), only to be called "Satan" moments later for trying to stop Jesus from going to Jerusalem (Matthew 16:23). Like many of us, Peter gets it, and then he doesn't get it.

One afternoon, several days into the retreat, I was taking a long walk among the rolling hills and tall trees of the retreat center. In some indeterminate place between mere imagination and ordinary reality, I found I was walking among the disciples with Peter at my side. It was the most vivid piece of acting imagination I had ever experienced. I knew without quite knowing how that Jesus was up ahead of us. "We" couldn't keep up even though we tried. All I could get were little glimpses of his back, just as Jesus turned corners or entered copses of trees. I looked to Peter, and it seemed to me that he shrugged, as if to say, "He's like that." I understood Peter was teaching me that Jesus is visible sometimes but always beyond our capacity to comprehend or control. We just follow by faith.

Another moment happened more recently. I was several days into the Camino, the ancient pilgrimage route in northern Spain. This particular morning my walking partner and I decided to get up early because we planned a long day of hiking over a small mountain range. We woke up in the dark, got bad coffee from a machine, and were soon on our way out of the village. It was so dark and foggy we used our headlamps to make sure we stayed on the path. After about half an hour, we found ourselves catching up to a small party of French people. They'd noticed us coming and stopped so they could help us negotiate a nearly impassable bog created by an overflowing cistern for sheep and cattle. With their flashlights and my minimal French, we were soon across the bog and on our way, our boots still dry. We thanked them and then, for a time, traveled together in silence, eyes focused ahead on the small patch of trail illuminated by our headlamps. And then I knew he was there. I could feel Jesus walking alongside me on my left-hand side. We walked along together for a time of silence. I said no word and heard no word, and did not desire one. It was enough to simply be with him on the way.

If you were to imagine that Jesus is with you right now, where would he appear? Would he be beside you, a companion on the way? Is he ahead of you, leading you along to an unknown destination? Is he behind you, holding you up in ways known and unknown? Or is he in front of you, holding you in his gaze, teaching or commissioning you for some work only you can do? Progress in humility requires the willingness to receive and affirm Jesus. He bids us to be toward him as James Merrill was with his friends: wax to receive and marble to retain.

Loving with the Holy Spirit

Scripture tells us that God is love (e.g., 1 John 4:16), so there is no virtue or action that will reveal the image and likeness of God more than when we love. We experience love in a variety of ways, from the love between friends to the love of parents for children and children for parents. But there is nothing more compelling and endlessly fascinating to us than what occurs between two people who fall in love and are subsequently called to mate for life. Jesus himself taps into this rich vein of human experience when he calls himself the bridegroom (Mark 2:19). We are to imagine that we are like a bride and that Jesus loves us and wants to be with us always. One way to learn about love, then, is to reflect on the stages of a loving married relationship.

Falling in love, with the overwhelming desire and excitement that often accompanies those first stages, is only part of the story of how we love, and so it is only part of the story of how our love reflects God's love. We know from scripture and from the stories of the saints that God's love for people and for communities can have an overwhelming beginning: The church remembers that Paul is knocked off his horse at the moment of his call, and the Bible tells us that the church is born with wind and tongues of flame. But in both the human and the divine spheres, falling in love is only the beginning. Our human capacity to love another person grows and matures over time. We are also called to commit to love and to stay in love.

I met Chloe during our first year of college. Both of us had arrived at school hoping to meet and date lots of people. However, we met each other within the first two weeks and, by the end of October, were together for life. How did this happen? Neither of us was looking for a spouse, and I had a girlfriend from home (who conveniently wrote me a "Dear John" letter that fall!) Yet somehow, we found that we were drawn so deeply to each other that within less than two months we had to name the reality that we were in love. At my suggestion and for ease of remembering, we named November first as the beginning of our relationship, although there was surely some moment earlier than that when we both knew we would be partners for life.

When I think back on how Chloe and I fell in love, I know it was not a question of rational choice. It was more like stumbling into a subterranean stream, a flow of water more powerful than I was. I did not know what was coming and could not clearly see where the stream was leading. It was like being carried forward in the dark. If I made any free choice in the matter, it was only to say "yes" and so trust the feelings I was having— and trust that Chloe, in some way, shared them.

As a priest, it has been my privilege to hear dozens of stories of how people met and fell in love. There is almost always an element of mystery in the way love enters our lives. We are carried along by something larger and more powerful than ourselves, something greater than either our memory can recall or our free choosing can control. We stumble into love in the fullness of time and our best reaction is only to say yes.

We are more active and deliberate when we take a second step by committing to love. One of the most significant moments in *The Book of Common Prayer* wedding service is during the exchange of the vows. The rubrics simply say, "The Man, facing the woman and taking her right hand in his, says…" and "Then they loose their hands and the Woman, still facing the man, takes his right hand in hers, and says…"[28] At wedding rehearsals, it's my experience that everyone, when practicing this part of the ceremony, wants to help out by meeting their partner halfway. But that's not what the rubric calls for. The rubric wants the man to take the woman, and the woman to allow herself to be taken. And then it wants the woman to take the man, and the man to allow himself to be taken. Ideally, each person must reach all the way across the space that separates the two people, take a nearly limp arm, and bring it to the middle. I find it always takes practice to get a couple to make this simple gesture.

In all likelihood, most of the rest of any couple's relationship will be filled with negotiation and compromise. They will meet in the middle. But in this moment, when each half of the couple is pledging for life, there is to be no compromise between them. Instead there are full and reciprocated gestures of taking and of being taken. Each must say only a moment later, "with all that I am and all that I have I honor you." In the giving and receiving of vows there is to be no reservation, no holding back, no negotiation. In the name of God, when we commit to love, we are to give ourselves completely.

Even here, the Spirit can work in unexpected ways. There is often an ineffable presence in a wedding ceremony that is hard to account for and of which we are barely aware. In my own wedding, it took my best man, Michael, to point out the Spirit's presence. At the beginning of the reception, I was a nervous wreck. I'm not a good dancer, and I had just married a gorgeous dancer. The thought of "leading" her in the first dance in front of a few hundred of our closest friends and family had me in knots. Just before the first dance, Michael got up to give the toast. As is often the tradition, he and I had been alone with the priest at the front of the church just before the wedding ceremony was to begin. In his toast, Michael talked about how nervous he had been at that moment but said that looking over at me he felt, exuding from me, a sense of total calm and certainty. It helped him and affirmed his sense that my marriage was going to be a good thing. It is odd to me, but Michael was right—even though I had not been conscious of it at the time of the ceremony. I knew I was about to make the most significant commitment of my life, and yet, by the gift of the Spirit—by the gift of something much larger than myself—I was calm. I was ready to give myself completely. (I wish I could report that I was as confident and self-assured on the dance floor. Our wedding video proves otherwise.)

But there is a third facet to love, and it is probably the most difficult. Staying in love over the remainder of a lifespan requires a different set of responses and skills from us than either falling in love or committing to it. Gordon Cosby, when reflecting on his years of leading communities in mission, said that it is easier to bring something into being than to keep it in being, true to itself.[29] So it is with our loving relationships.

Even the strongest marriages can be like fine bottles of red wine. Young, untried wines go through three stages. In the first few years, they can be attractive and fruity but with a somewhat unpleasant taste. The right kind of unpleasant taste, either an extra acidic bite or a roughness on the tongue, are characteristics that demonstrate that the wine could age well.

Often, these same wines enter a second stage and close down for a few years. This means that the delightful flavor of the first stage is gone, but the profound flavors of maturity have not yet emerged. The wine can be boring and even slightly unpleasant. So it often is with love. Sometimes, particularly at first, love demands that we allow ourselves to be swept along in its exuberance, like the fun fruitiness of a young wine. Other times, often later in the relationship, the relationship can seem to close down and so love consists in the decision to just keep showing up, choosing to be faithful to the one we love even when it is dull and seems to have lost its flavor. Sometimes, especially at first, it seems love is beyond our will. At other times, if love is to stay alive, it requires our will. I mean this not in the sense of forcing love—willing it into something, but in the sense of the decision made time and again to be attentive, respectful, and even obedient.

A good wine then enters into its third and most glorious phase. Some of the appealing fruitiness of the first phase is lost, but it is replaced with depth and subtlety. A good, well-aged wine unfolds in the mouth and awareness for as long as a minute, with great pleasure for all. Long-term studies of marital satisfaction show that if couples can successfully negotiate the stresses and strains of the middle stages of their relationship, often accompanied by the challenges of childrearing, they will enter the last stages with marital satisfaction that is actually higher than when they first fell in love. Just as the full enjoyment over time of a great bottle of wine requires patience and proper care, so it is with our loving relationships.

Through the course of a long relationship, we will inevitably experience temptations to be unfaithful in various ways. There are many ways to be unfaithful that fall short of adultery. We may check out of challenging conversations necessary to keep a relationship vital, or we may allow work or hobbies to consume too much of our time and energy. Other relationships with children, work colleagues, or friends may take too much precedence. The practice of staying faithful to our partner is a profoundly spiritual one. The practice consists

The Image of God

in remembering every day to treat the other as what we knew him or her to be right from the start, an unfathomable gift of love.

I think of a couple I see often. My drive to work takes me past the Mission of San Rafael, a Roman Catholic Church on the site of one of the original Franciscan mission outposts in California. Often I am driving past just as the morning mass is letting out. When the timing is right, I always see an older couple walking away from the church, holding hands. Their walk is relaxed with a slight, energetic bounce. I look at their hands, and I feel sacred envy. Their hands are a symbol to me of love maintained and strengthened over the course of a lifetime. One of Augustine's attempts to point to the mystery of the Trinity helps explain my deep reaction. "Love means someone loving and something loved with love. There you are with three, the lover, what is being loved, and love."[30] The two halves of the couple are the lover and the one being loved. Those held hands are the love itself, nurtured over a lifetime of love.

I've never met the couple, and if I did, I am certain I would hear of both joy and suffering. If I really came to know them well, I might even hear of times of great kindness and grace as well as times of frustration and even petty cruelty. I believe this to be true because of my own experience and because of the teaching of the church. Chloe and I have been very blessed in our relationship, but our life together has not gone unmarred by selfishness and meanness. In fact I believe part of why we are together is to slowly unlearn some of the selfishness we both brought into the relationship and so, over time, learn to truly love.

Finding A Spiritual Friend and Guide

The good news is that we are not meant to be alone in this work of the fifth step of claiming the image and likeness of God. Again, Benedict writes that a monk "does not conceal from his abbot any sinful thoughts entering his heart, or any wrongs committed in secret, but rather confesses them humbly" (THE RULE OF SAINT BENEDICT, 7:44). Most of us don't have abbots, but all of us have access to people who can play the role of spiritual confidant. This aspect of our spiritual growth requires someone we trust. The work we do on ourselves, by ourselves, will always reach a limit. We need others to help us to distinguish the path of love from the path of deceit. There are two characteristics of speaking truthfully. First, we honestly face into where we have erred and get into the practice of confessing our sins. Second, we learn to discover and claim our real gifts and offer them for the world.

Speaking truthfully about our sin is no easy matter. It requires holding steady in the face of some powerful shame. There is something in us that would prefer to continue in a falsehood we have always clung to rather than to let it go and continue on the path of truth. It is mortifying to admit to ourselves and, even more, to others that we have been deceived. We are like Fonzie from the old TV show *Happy Days*. We think we are cool and in control, but when the truth comes out, we can barely begin to articulate what is true. Like Fonzie, we begin to speak and what comes out is like an old, underused engine trying to start "I was wr… I was wr… I was wr… ."[31]

Augustine, as is often the case, precisely captures the core of our dilemma. "We love the truth when it enlightens but

The Image of God

hate it when it accuses. Because we do not want to be deceived and do want to deceive, we love truth when it reveals itself and hate it when it reveals us."[32] If we return to the exercise at the beginning of the book where someone stares into our eyes and asks, "Who are you really?" a significant part of the truth is actions, thoughts, and stances for which we are or ought to be ashamed. The rare moment when someone looks deeply in our eyes includes great promise but also terror. We hunger to be known. And we are afraid to be known.

This fifth step, then, holds great potential. Either we will continue the spiritual journey in a greater knowledge of the truth of ourselves and of God, or we will stay where we are, cloaked in falsehood or deception. Spiritual master and Trappist monk Michael Casey states it precisely: "Taking the difficult step of speaking frankly about oneself is the price one pays for spiritual progress beyond a certain point. Encouragingly, it is also the sign that one has already made considerable advance in opening oneself to the workings of grace."[33]

We all need help at this step. We need a safe relationship with another who can act as our spiritual midwife in the process. Much of the work is ours: we must engage in the hard but simple act of speaking truthfully about ourselves without flinching and without excusing ourselves. No one else can recast our core self-perception so that the image we have of ourselves is free of distorting lies and concealing excuses. The primary role of the other is to simply hold us in love and keep confidence, telling no one what has been disclosed. Simply keeping confidence is often enough.

There may also be a word of advice that is offered in response to our confession. Almost always a word or two is all we can take. Most often our sin is like a splinter in the flesh. Over time the resulting infection and not the splinter itself causes most of the pain. Confession is often a process by which the splinter can be removed and revealed as the small, pathetic object it so often is. Only then can the healing begin.

Stability is one of the keys to a healthy relationship with a spiritual friend or director. Over time, trust deepens, and we find that we can speak more truthfully about ourselves. The other develops the ability to both detect and point out how we are deceiving ourselves. Over the course of a lifetime we may hope to have a handful of these guides and confidants.

Our goal is simply to get into and maintain a daily habit of thinking and speaking truthfully about ourselves. Just as we visit a doctor only occasionally but are faced each day with choices that either lead to health or sickness, so it is with our souls. Speaking truthfully about ourselves, particularly if we always keep in mind the beauty and power of the divine image in us, is a reminder that we do not need to settle for anything less than full spiritual health.

Saint Paul, in his hymn to love, reminds us that in this mortal life "we see in a mirror, dimly" (1 Corinthians 13:12). As in all things, the full truth about ourselves is known only to God. But thanks to spiritual masters like Benedict and Augustine we can confidently explore parts of ourselves, seeking glimpses of the divine image. In this chapter, inspired by Augustine, I've invited you to play with the idea that we are one and three like God is one and three. In the way we remember, in the way we make friends, and in the way we love, we can catch glimpses, by grace, of our true selves, made in the image of God. We can see sketches of the master artist's true intention for us.

Once we have a clearer sense of what in us is the true image of God and what is the distorting likeness, we are ready to move to the most difficult steps in Benedict's ladder of humility. In steps six through eight, life invites us to release any sense of superiority, and any excessive sense of control and autonomy. The distorting likeness is stripped away so that more of the true and beautiful image and likeness can emerge.

Chapter 5

Stripping

6. Releasing Superiority
7. Releasing Control
8. Releasing Autonomy

Most of the work of restoring *The Last Supper* was in carefully stripping away almost everything that wasn't painted by Leonardo. There was much to remove. In addition to dirt and pollution, seven previous restorations left layers of materials. There were hard resins from 1903, soft resins from 1924, and shellac from 1947. There was a particular shade of yellow that didn't exist until 1625 and so must have been from a later repainting. There were layers of wax beneath Jesus that refused to yield to any chemical treatment and so needed to be removed mechanically.[34]

Special care was given to the faces, all of which had their own issues. Simon and Matthew were in particularly bad shape. Simon's profile was coarsely delineated by later re-paintings. His expressive features were weighed down and the top of his head was anatomically incorrect. Matthew's mouth had been reduced to a bitter and vulgar expression and, inexplicably, he was given a beard where Leonardo intended no such thing.[35]

Leonardo took great care to give each face a unique expression and character, based on his careful observation of the people of fifteenth-century Milan. If the world was ever going to see what Leonardo intended, all of this accretion needed to be carefully stripped away.

Similarly, each of us has a face that was created uniquely by God in God's own image. Because of the unique way we were created, because of what has happened to us in life (and, unlike images in a painting, because of choices we have made), our whole image is not apparent to the world. I began this book by sharing the scriptural understanding that we are each made in the "image and likeness" of God. An ancient way to interpret that phrase is to claim that the "image" is indestructible because it is a sheer gift from God that can never be taken away. The "likeness" is all the ways that God intends us to be good, true, and beautiful as God is good, true, and beautiful. We have each failed to achieve our full potential and so fail to show forth our genuine likeness of God to the world. Like the faces in *The Last Supper* in the 1970s, our image and likeness has deteriorated and been covered over.

Sins That Obscure God's Image

We each have our own unique stories of deterioration. But the wisdom of the Christian tradition is that our likenesses to God tend to deteriorate in some similar patterns. The most memorable ancient description of our well-worn patterns of self-destruction is the seven deadly sins. Although the list is not in the Bible, it has been a useful spiritual tool since the early centuries of the church. In the western tradition, the most famous list of seven comes from the middle part of

Dante's *Divine Comedy*, the *Purgatorio*. In that central part of the poem, the souls of the dead are being purged of their earthly sin on their way to Paradise.

In each of the three parts of the *Comedy*, Dante must travel through a portion of the afterworld shaped to reflect the spiritual state of the souls he encounters. The first part, the *Inferno*, is in the deep pit of hell. The souls in hell are forever stuck in a pit, telling their self-justifying tales. The final part, the *Paradiso*, is in the celestial spheres where souls are forever dancing and singing God's praises, caught up in the bliss of the heavenly banquet. The middle portion, the *Purgatorio*, is on a seven-storied mountain. The souls in Purgatory are steadily working up the stories of the mountain with their hearts firmly fixed on going toward God. On each story of this mountain, these souls destined for Paradise are cleansed of the different sorts of sins they indulged in during their earthly lives. The seven stages of the mountain in order are pride, envy, wrath, sloth, gluttony, greed, and lust.

By the time Dante arrives at the mountain of Purgatory, he has already received the assurance that after his death he will eventually end up in Paradise. However, he will not be one of the precious few who go directly to Paradise and so skip the process of purification in Purgatory. After death, Dante must first be cleansed of the sins that marred his earthly life. As he travels up the seven stories of the mountain of Purgatory, it becomes clear to him that, after he dies, there are three areas where he will need to spend extra time. Pride, wrath, and lust all afflicted the earthly Dante and made him less than he otherwise might have been. And so, for a period of time in the afterlife, Dante will join the other souls in circling pride, the first story of the mountain, with a heavy rock on his back so that he can learn humility. He will circle the third story of wrath, blinded by smoke until he masters meekness. He will burn in the seventh and final story of lust until his earthly desire is transformed into a pure love of God.

Along with Augustine, Dante is clear that God refuses to be embraced alongside anything false, bad, or ugly. All of these must be left behind if we want to spend eternity with God. Purgatory is Dante's imaginative picture of the process by which God makes us worthy to be with God forever alongside all the other saints and the angels. In the book, Dante has the spiritual maturity to acknowledge the specific ways that the image and likeness of God have been corrupted in him. Further, he can imagine the sort of cleansing process he will need to endure in Purgatory if he is going to be made worthy to be with God. We can imagine that by the time Dante has traveled up the mountain of Purgatory his image of God will be revealed and his likeness fully restored.

If we wish to reveal more of our divine beauty in this life, Dante gives us a great guiding principle. Of the seven deadly sins, we are likely to be particularly susceptible to three. One mark of spiritual maturity is to be able to name our three greatest areas of sin out of this ancient list of seven. Further, if we are available and alert, we may notice God provides us ways to be purged and cleansed even in this life of our most tempting and sticky sins.

For myself I have come to see that one of my most prominent sins is envy, or "discontent and resentment aroused by desire for the possessions or qualities of another."[36] While I have little envy for the possessions of others, I have been afflicted with the nagging sense that my inherent qualities are insufficient. I have felt that if I only had the qualities I perceive in certain others around me, I would finally be loved, admired, and respected. I have been at times unable to rest in the reality that God can rejoice in me just as God intended me to be. As a result, I have restlessly cast my eyes about, and with great discontent, tried and failed to assume the qualities of another.

To be restored to the image and likeness of God in this life, I needed to be stripped of the sin of envy like the faces of Simon, Matthew, and the other apostles in *The Last Supper* were stripped of gunk and the distorted restorations of the ages. As we go into a time of stripping, we are all as the eleventh-century theologian and Archbishop Saint Anselm describes himself in one of his prayers:

> I acknowledge, Lord, and I give thanks that You have created Your image in me, so that I may remember You, think of You, love You. But this image is so effaced and worn away by vice, so darkened by the smoke of sin, that it cannot do what it was made to do unless You renew it and reform it.[37]

I believe that, when the time was ripe, God, like a master restorer, chose to strip me of much of my sin of envy—a sin that, like smoke, had darkened the shining beauty of God's image and likeness in me. Reading, reflecting, and praying on these next three steps of humility held me steady through a time of God's renewal and reformation.

My Refiner's Fire

I knew for certain I was in a time of deep trial because of a dream. At the time I had the dream, I was in my mid-thirties and living in Los Angeles. In the dream, I was walking along a path by the ocean about halfway down a cliff. There was a cave and I walked inside it. At the back of the cave was a body in a bathtub. It was my body, and it was suspended above the bottom of the tub by fishhooks embedded throughout my flesh and held taut by a line to the side of the tub. When I woke up from the dream and tried to understand its meaning for my life, I knew my task was to remove the metaphorical fishhooks, get out of the tub, get out of the cave, and keep walking.

The words that kept me centered as I tried to escape the cave in my dream came from a commentary on these next steps. Michael Casey wrote, "the one who seeks nothing else but God progressively finds what he seeks. First he finds nothing else, then he finds God."[38] I proceeded by faith that his words were true.

My time in the cave had begun with a phone call that came to me out of the blue. I was in my office at my church in Connecticut when I got a surprise call from the head priest of a well-known church in Los Angeles. I had been looking for a place where I could spend most of my energy on attracting my GenX peers to church, and this appeared to be that opportunity. This priest cast a wonderful vision of what her church was, what it could become, and what my role might be. It was exciting, and a wonderful and inspiring vision of a thriving church.

A visit to Los Angeles with Chloe, who is from Southern California, confirmed how attractive and vibrant the church was, and I soon committed to serving there. A few months later, I drove our car alone across the country while Chloe finished up her work on the East Coast. It was a quiet and centering time, filled with visits to good friends and family along the way. The only sour note was a sinking feeling in my stomach as I came off the high desert on Route 15 and into the Los Angeles basin. At a deep level, I already knew I was going to be facing a stern test.

All went very well at first. My first sermon seemed to be a great hit with parishioners. Much to my surprise, I loved being in Los Angeles and remember showing up to work one day on the Santa Monica Boulevard in my collar and some brand-new stretch black jeans and feeling like the coolest priest in the entire Anglican Communion.

Over two years later, a shift began. One element in the shift was the ordinary life cycle of parish programs and my own professional development. Who I was and the work I was called to do were starting to change from a focus on people my own age to teaching the Christian disciplines to people of all ages. Much more painful and confusing, however, was a shift in the staff dynamics. Another associate had arrived on the staff. He was demographically similar to me but had a very different set of gifts.

At first I welcomed his addition and imagined that it would help create a kind of "dream team" among the senior staff of the parish. I thought we would accomplish great things together. Instead, in my envious eyes, he slowly became a rival and competitor, and I always seemed to lose by comparison. I could only see how others seemed to admire his qualities and disregard my own.

I tried to press on as though things hadn't really changed that much. I assumed the situation would eventually shift back to the joy and energy I had felt in my first two years there. Meanwhile, my poor body and imagination took on the strain. My back was almost continually a mess of painful knots. I would perform most of my duties with an inner sense of emptiness, and my attempts at friendship and connection failed repeatedly as others seemed to prefer the company of the rival to me. I felt removed even from the activities that used to give me the deepest pleasure. I remember once looking on at a contemplative evening worship service of music and silence, beauty and calm, and feeling as though I were trapped under a sheet of ice gazing up at clean air and blue skies but drowning. It was then that I had the dream of the fishhooks. The fishhooks seemed to me all the ways my situation had hooked me. I knew I needed to get out.

I went into therapy hoping for full insight, but I never got it. The therapist, who was a very wise and spiritually grounded Christian, counted me as one of her success stories simply because she helped me escape. After five years of service in Los Angeles, I left to become the head of my own church, which was a small, lovely, struggling community just north of San Francisco. For a time, I had to be content with fragments and glimpses of grace and truth. I had been stripped, but I didn't know exactly how or why.

Step Six:
Releasing Superiority

content with the lowest

— The Rule of Saint Benedict, 7:49

Reflection on step six helped me begin to get deeper insight. It is, in its entirety, "that a monk is content with the lowest and most menial treatment, and regards himself as a poor and worthless workman in whatever task he is given, saying to himself with the prophet I am insignificant and ignorant, no better than a beast before you, yet I am with you always." (The Rule of Saint Benedict, 7:49) I knew all along that I needed to be careful with this step. Self-abnegation is very close to self-hatred, which is itself a sin. The process of diminishment is dangerous. An ancient piece of ethical advice is to remember that discretion is the mother of all virtues. Discretion is never more critical than when we find ourselves in the midst of these steps. The challenge is to accept the suffering without either lashing out in unjust anger at others or folding into an acidic self-loathing.

I needed to get out of the cave before I could begin learning the wisdom of my time trapped in misery in Southern California. Some time after I left the church, one big piece of the puzzle fell into place. I finally came to grips with the fact that I suffered from envy. The harsh language of this step, for example that one is to think of oneself as "poor" and "worthless," absolutely undermines envy. If we don't have an inflated ego around anything we do, comparisons with others are not a problem. The sign that we are maturing gracefully is contentment with who we are and what we have accomplished. The scriptural quote in this step ends with the psalm writer's clear confidence that he is always with God, and that is enough.

The contentment from this step eluded me, even years after leaving the Los Angeles congregation. I was still plagued by envy of others. With some trepidation, I headed back east to take a class in English spirituality. The class was taught by a seminary classmate who had become a professor of theology at a seminary. Now that I finally acknowledged that I was under the power of envy, I expected to struggle the entire time I was taking the course since my classmate's career was thriving. However, I found that it was not at all the case. Here was a man who was accomplishing everything I could have hoped for had I followed my gifts and passion in a slightly different direction. Yet, unlike my time in Los Angeles, I felt no envy. In fact, I felt genuinely delighted for him. Why?

When I was in Los Angeles, I simply wasn't confident in who I was. I hadn't yet learned that I am lovable just as I was made. As a result, I was often driven to try to be the person others wanted me to be. I held onto the idea that others wished I was someone else: more charming and sociable, less intellectual and passionate. I believed my rival had those qualities, and it ate me up that I lacked them. My envy led me to believe things that were simply false.

I was caught in a trap, too dependent on what others thought of me. The primary sin in all this sprang from my unarticulated expectation that I was going to be loved by others as though I was the most important person in the world. I believed I needed to be superior, assuming all possible gifts, in order to be fully loved. Words from the poet W.H. Auden capture so much of what drove me at the time. He says that the error in each man and woman "Comes from what it cannot have/Not Universal love/But to be loved alone."

In Los Angeles, I was serving a parish filled with people in the movie industry. So many wanted to be stars—to "be loved alone." Yet they were almost always extras or, at best, playing secondary parts. Like them, I needed to learn that I was ordinary and not a star.

On the mountain of Purgatory, the souls on the story of envy have their eyes sewn shut. They can no longer cast their eyes about restlessly but must focus inward. They sit side by side, their backs against the mountain and their heads resting on each other's shoulders. They are humble companions in the all-important task of becoming themselves, as God intended them to be. God for a time mercifully seals their eyes so that they can train their perception inwards, where God has given each soul all that is needed.

Through the suffering I experienced at that church and the struggle toward healing afterward, I became more who I am. I became less significant and less superior and so more nearly a person. I am neither a star nor a golden boy. I am simply human and—like all others—made in the image and likeness of God. That is enough. There is no reason to cast my eyes about in envy.

This has been the story of one person's struggle with just one of the seven deadly sins. There is no one story that will be true of everyone. We each have our own peculiar faults, and no one can force us to mend those faults that are deep in our hearts. We each have to go through our own process of releasing our own, often fearful, sense of superiority and of embracing our own humble yet beautiful identity as an ordinary human being. What Benedict saw so accurately is that we often need to ask ourselves, as we are going through a time of trial, if the pains we are experiencing are ultimately for our own good. Just because a process hurts does not mean that it is not an expression of God's love for us.

Step Seven:
Releasing Control

a blessing that you have humbled me
so that I can learn your commandments
—The Rule of Saint Benedict, 7:54

The contrast between my first two years in Los Angeles and my last three rings true with one of the central observations in step seven. Spiritual growth is never steady and uninterrupted. There are good times, and there are bad times, and we have almost no control over this often disorienting fluctuation. We must expect the changes in fortune and then trust that God is in the midst of it all. Step seven concludes with Benedict quoting twice from the psalms. Psalm 88 reads, "I was exalted, then I was humbled and overwhelmed with confusion" (16). Psalm 119 notes that "It is a blessing that you have humbled me so that I can learn your commandments" (71, 73). In highlighting these psalms, Benedict communicates that we can expect times of exaltation and then times of confusion. Through both, we are called to release control and trust that God is slowly revealing to us God's own ways, so often different from our own.

One who never lost sight of both the reality of our changeable fortunes or the truth of God's steadfast love was Bernard of Clairvaux, an eleventh-century follower of Benedict. Bernard knew that life is difficult and filled with trials and suffering, and also that life is sweet and filled with joy and great consolations. Both of these things are true, and no one is immune from the former or utterly locked out of the latter.

A central teaching of Bernard was what he called *vicissitudo* and is often translated as alternation. He used the word to describe a wide range of experiences of a faithful Christian. On a grand level, alternation means the way a Christian experiences alternation between God's mercy and God's judgment. Bernard imagines that he is kneeling at Jesus' feet as he worships him and embraces one foot and then the other. He notices that if he stays too much on the foot of mercy, he grows slack, but if he stays too long on the foot of judgment, he is paralyzed in terror. On the earthly pilgrimage, he must have both feet to help him walk until, at the end of time or the end of his life, mercy makes its final triumph over judgment. For now, in this life, our experience of Jesus must alternate between mercy and judgment if we wish to live in truth.[39]

On a daily basis, alternation means that for even the most faithful follower of Jesus, the reality of God falls in and out of our attention. He writes, "this process of Alternation goes on all the time…the just one falls seven times and seven times gets up again…he sees himself falling and knows when he has fallen and wants to get up again and calls out for a helping hand, saying, 'O Lord, at your will you made me splendid in virtue, but then you turned away your face and I was overcome.'"[40] The faithful one alternates between standing and falling but always asks for help.

Whether it is on the grand level or on a daily basis, the experience of alternation is meant to increase our love. Consider the story of the road to Emmaus. Jesus, his identity

Stripping

hidden, walks alongside his disciples and teaches them. Then "as they came near the village to which they were going, he walked ahead as if he were going on. But they urged him strongly, saying 'Stay with us'" (Luke 24:28-9). This story can be viewed as an example of the way God works with our hearts by being with us and then seeming to pull away. God knows that absence makes the heart grow fonder. Above all, God wants lovers whose hearts are always growing in love.

Like many monks of his era, Bernard was drawn deeply to the Song of Songs with its poetry of secular love between a man and a woman transposed into a religious context. His greatest work is a series of eighty sermons on the Song of Songs. (And he only got as far as the beginning of the third chapter out of eight!) His imagination is filled with the notion of God wooing us like a passionate lover. His desire inflames ours, and our desire grows as our experience alternates between God's presence and absence. In one of his greatest sermons, Bernard confesses that God frequently visits his soul. He writes:

> And so when the Bridegroom, the Word, came to me he never made any sign that he was coming; there was no sound of his voice, no glimpse of his face, no footfall. There was no movement of his by which I could know his coming; none of my senses showed me that he had flooded the depths of my being. Only by the warmth of my heart, as I said before, did I know he was there, and I knew the power of his might because my faults were purged and my body's yearnings brought under control...But when the Word has left me, and all these things become dim and weak and cold, as though you had taken the fire from under a boiling pot, I know that he has gone. Then my soul cannot help being sorrowful until he returns, and my heart grows warm within me, and I know he is there.[41]

Perhaps, like Jesus with his followers on the road to Emmaus, God parts company from us not to punish us but to increase our capacity for love. He wishes us to cry out with all the passion of a lover, "Stay with us!"

Maybe God wanted me to know the tenderness, heartache, and beauty of love in a deeper way than I was capable of in my mid-thirties. Maybe I was allowed to get trapped under ice and suspended by fishhooks so that, immobilized and frozen as I was, I could cry, from a most vulnerable place where I had no control, "God help me! I need you! Only you can save me!"

Step Eight:
Releasing Autonomy

does only what is endorsed by the common rule
—The Rule of Saint Benedict, 7:55

The eighth step of humility is an intensification of membership in community. The process of membership begins in earlier steps, particularly in practicing sacred obedience where we learn the disciplines of joining a church, becoming friends with the poor, and committing ourselves to a Discipleship Group. In step four, cultivating patience, the process deepens as we train our hearts to quietly embrace suffering. Step eight is a complete reliance on the hard-earned wisdom of community and tradition. It is, in its entirety, "that a monk does only what is endorsed by the common rule of the monastery and the example set by his superiors" (The Rule of Saint Benedict, 7:55).

This step emphasizes the truth that God made us as social creatures. Since the early centuries of the church, there have been two ways to understand that we are made in the image of God, the Three in One. When we explored the fifth step—knowing ourselves as God's image, we looked at how each of us individually is made in the image of God the Trinity and how the Three in One is reflected in our capacities to remember, receive, and love. But tradition has also taught that we are made in the image of God when we are together. The wisdom of the church is that the three persons of the Trinity are always and eternally loving each other. It is impossible to really picture what this means because God is beyond our imaginations, but many have tried to understand the social dynamic of God's love as a kind of movement. Perhaps it is akin to a dance, where each person of the Trinity is constantly loving the others completely, to the point of emptiness, and at the same time receiving love completely, to the point of overflowing. I picture a hydraulic system where the water is never still but always in motion.

We are called to love others with similar abandonment, trust, and generosity. It would be sweet if it were our natural state to love so completely. It is the greatest sadness imaginable that we are so very far from giving and receiving love in this way. We live in original sin and are always doing things that make matters worse. Our image and likeness keep getting ruined and covered over. By grace we humans have developed various ways to bind ourselves to one another so that love is more likely to flow freely, allowing us to show forth our true selves. As I experienced my time of trial, I was held up by loving people in a living tradition. In particular, I was borne up by my parish church, my wife, and a group of clergy colleagues. What sustained me was not just the love and support of each of these people, but the reality that each of them was bound to me in Christian covenant.

The large church—where I learned my hardest lessons—was a Christian community where Jesus was Lord, and that saved me. I was not alone in the raw human struggle to know God and make God the center of my life. I was bound to a community of other people traveling well-worn paths alongside me into the heart of God. I knew we were all brothers and sisters at the deepest level because of the powerful unifying sacrament of baptism. Ritually, we had all died to our old selves and been born again into the family of God, the household of faith, the body of Christ. Even the rival and I were made one in Jesus the moment we were baptized.

To my wife, I was bound in Christ until death in the covenant of marriage. On July 11, 1992 at the beginning of our wedding ceremony, the priest asked each of us if we would love, comfort, honor, and keep each other in sickness and in health and be faithful as long as we both live. We both said yes. Later, I looked into Chloe's eyes and said, "I give you this ring as a symbol of my vow, and with all that I am and all that I have, I honor you, in the Name of the Father, and of the Son, and of the Holy Spirit."[42] And she said the same to me. When my time of trial came, bound by our vows, she stood faithfully by my side.

The men in my clergy colleague group all shared the bond of the vows of ordination. We had each made vows to "labor together... with (our) fellow ministers to build up the family of God."[43] When we began our group of nine colleagues, we made a further commitment to each other to meet twice a year to support and love one another until death. A few years after we began the group, we had a horrific fight at the dinner table at a spring meeting. We were fighting over precisely the things that divide the church now, namely sexuality, restraint, and the obligations we have to keep one another virtuous. Later, we all noted how close we had come to breaking apart that night. What kept us together in that moment was that one of us, precisely as things seemed to be falling apart, said, "Remember, we have all put on Christ."

Each of these vows is an outward symbol of the inward spiritual reality that I am rooted, in a number of ways, to the community of people going back to the first people who gathered around Jesus. I am religious, not merely spiritual. The origin of the word "religious" is to be bound. I was bound to these others and so could be held as I endured a season of cleansing pain that I could not have endured alone, operating out of rules I had to make up as I went along. I needed the common rules of the tradition to help me through. I know I would have flinched, fleeing like the disciples on Good Friday, had I not been bound through these vows to community in Jesus.

Viewed in this way, and only with the benefit of time and hindsight, perhaps that bathtub in the cave was both tomb and womb. Maybe some of those ties were like the vows that held me in place while God did the necessary stripping. I had to die so that I might be made alive again in Christ.

Working on Our Belovedness

This chapter is the story of one of the Seven Deadly Sins in one person's life and how God seemed to gradually strip the sins by guiding me to release superiority, control, and autonomy. The same dynamics can be applied to other people and to the other sins of pride, wrath, sloth, greed, gluttony, and lust. Beneath each of these self-willed distortions of the image of God lies the toxic misuse of our gift of free will. Humility requires that we slowly find ways to overcome our fears and hand ourselves over to God's greatness, providence, and all-embracing love. We allow God's will to reform and replace our own. In these steps we learn to trust God's work of renewal and reformation, even and especially when it is painful and disorienting.

Above all we must each find ways to constantly remember God's love. In the midst of my time of trial, at precisely the time I felt trapped by fishhooks, another seed was planted for my salvation. In the fall of 2003, I made my first visit to the Church of the Saviour, the high-commitment ecumenical church in Washington, D.C. that I discussed in an earlier chapter. The highlight was a short talk by lead pastor Gordon Cosby where he shared the distilled wisdom of his seventy years in active ministry. He described about a half dozen elements that needed to be in place if a Christian community was going to have authenticity and depth. One element was that every member of the community had to confront the things inside him or herself that blocked them from intimacy with others. He said that as part of that process of learning intimacy, each person "needed to be working on his or her belovedness."[44]

At the end of the talk, he invited questions. My hand shot up in the air. I wanted to know what it meant to "work on belovedness." Before I had the opportunity to speak, he qualified his invitation and said, "not the hard questions, no one has answers to those." My hand slowly went down. I knew my question had no easy answer. But the seed had been planted. In the midst of my time of trial, I learned that God and I needed to work on my sense that I, too, was God's beloved child. I am beloved for precisely the good qualities God has already given me. The same thing is true of you.

By God's grace, and only by God's grace, I believe that what God loves in me is more apparent to the world now than it was when I was in that time of trial. God has stripped me of some gunk and so what God created in me can now be more clearly seen.

Likewise, the process of carefully stripping *The Last Supper* revealed Leonardo's beautiful initial intentions for

Simon and Matthew. For centuries viewers saw that Simon, who is at the right end of the table, was in receding profile and so looking down the length of the table to Bartholomew at the other end. This was not accurate. Leonardo created Simon's face in profile, looking slightly away from the viewer so that he is turned toward his neighbor Thaddeus. The church remembers that Simon and Thaddeus were martyred together. Perhaps Leonardo intended us to see the two of them in a moment that sealed their friendship.

Matthew's face gained new life by the restoration. His lips were restored to a soft fleshiness just opening in amazement at Jesus' announcement that one of them would betray him. His eyes acquired a new vivacity in their startled gaze, and the recovery of some of the smoky quality of Leonardo's art on his cheeks gave his face plasticity and softness. Finally, without the beard and with the restoration of the original lines, it was clear that Leonardo had given him the classic profile of a young aristocrat from ancient Rome. The loving hands of the restorers revealed truth, beauty, relationship, and dignity.[45]

These steps of releasing superiority, control, and autonomy are steps six through eight of our own restoration project, not the beginning. They only make sense in Jesus and in love if we are building on a very solid foundation of faith built over time. Now at this stage, personality can die, or at least begin its death throes, and true personhood can emerge. The scab can fall off, and the tender, beautiful, lively, flesh can be exposed without fear of annihilation.

Once, when I was driving through the clotted traffic of west Los Angeles, a phrase bubbled up into my mind that sounded familiar, but I couldn't quite place it. I wanted to believe it was scripture but wasn't entirely sure. When I reached my office, I spent part of the morning looking for it and soon found it in the third chapter of Colossians. It says simply, "your life is hidden with Christ in God" (3). As you endure your own alienation from sin and try to exit your cave safely, keep returning to these words: Your life is hidden with Christ. This is true because of the external bonds that have connected you to him. If you look to him first, you will be safe, you will be loved.

It will not always be easy. In any given Christian community, as in every family, there will never be enough support, respect, and admiration to go around. The human love that is available, tainted or untainted, will always outstrip the need. Always, always, always. But, as Michael Casey put it so precisely, our neediness is the counterpoint to the divine abundance.[46] Christian communities become effective when we regard with total seriousness the ties that bind us together in Jesus and allow his love to work through us. This is the only way. We do not need to feel alone; neither do we need to earn any sense of belonging. As we are stripped of our illusions of superiority, control, and autonomy, God reveals the grace of true community grounded in God's love.

Mature humility emerges as we realize that the love that holds us to each other does not come from us. Not only are we not its source, we do not control it. More often than not, as we grow in humility we become less aware of how love has emerged from us and touched the lives of others. Part of Benedict's insight is that the less we think about our impact on others, and the less we try to control that impact, the more the divine love emerges from us for the sake of others. If we want to be people of love we must learn to be quiet and vigilant. And so we soon move on to the final four steps.

CHAPTER 6

Quiet Self-Mastery

9. Being Quiet on Purpose
10. Being Quiet from our Depths
11. Being Quiet and Gentle
12. Being Vigilant

In the end, the restoration of *The Last Supper* was fragile and incomplete. Some of the underlying flaws of the painting, which had been present since the beginning, could not be fully corrected. In some areas of the painting, the restorers decided to keep some of the former restorations, just so there could be some semblance of Leonardo's original intention. In other areas, they filled in blank spots with easily removable washes of watercolor. Presenting to the world an image as faithful as possible to the work of the master meant accepting and even protecting incompletion and fragility.

The same is true of us. In this life, what can be accomplished in our project of restoration has its limits. Our progress will always feel—and in fact will be—quite fragile. The world is not set up to guarantee us permanent bliss in this life. Any progress that we make in revealing the image and likeness of God can be quickly and easily undone, even in a moment. Some of the earliest images of the steps of humility show monks at the very top of a ladder, about to be embraced by Jesus, only to be dragged back down by little demons. Under stress, we all regress.

In Quietness and Trust Will Be Our Strength

Jesus warns us that the world will never be our true home. He tells us that he is not of this world, and that, if we are following him, we can expect seasons and times of rejection, abuse, pain, and misunderstanding. On his last night, he teaches his followers,

> If the world hates you, be aware that it hated me before it hated you. If you belonged to the world, the world would love you as its own. Because you do not belong to the world, but I have chosen you out of the world— therefore the world hates you. Remember the word that I said to you, 'Servants are not greater than their master.' If they persecuted me, they will persecute you (John 15:18-20a).

As followers of Jesus, we can expect that the world will not always be kind to us.

Neither has the world been kind to *The Last Supper*. There are some new structures in place to help prevent future abuse of the painting. Recently I was able to fulfill a childhood dream and see the painting in person. We had been instructed to arrive twenty minutes early and so found ourselves waiting with twenty other people from around the world in an outer chamber. At our precise ticketed time, a guide took us through two different sealed chambers with automatic sliding doors. The strict schedule and the holding pens are a sterile, dehumanizing way to approach a humanist masterpiece. The painting has been well protected but at the cost of spontaneity and intimacy.

In our own efforts to stand firm against a corrupting world, we can't be so freeze-dried. In fact, we are called to just the opposite. As former Archbishop of Canterbury and theologian Rowan Williams has put it, "a Christian is called to have more exposed nerves, not less."[47] Yet, like *The Last Supper,* we need to fend off the attacks and atmospheric pollution of a world that wants to cover and corrupt our beauty and truth, the image of God in which we were created. These last steps of humility teach, along with the prophet Isaiah, that "in quietness and trust shall be your strength" (30:15).

So often greatness in life is about being strong and still. A perfect example is the shift in the character of Jacob, the great patriarch who had the dream that inspired Benedict to refine these twelve steps we are following. In the middle part of the book of Genesis, Jacob is a wily and engaging character, out for himself and his own gain. He outwits his brother and his employer, dreams a great dream, and finally wrestles with an angel. He is an active man, leading a life filled with adventure. At the end of his last major exploit, grappling with the divine figure, he is renamed Israel. In that moment, he becomes a true patriarch and so exists no longer for himself alone but for the nation he must father.

As the story moves forward, Jacob shifts to a supporting role. He may be secondary to the action, but he is essential as a deliverer of blessing. The experience of fatherhood has stripped Jacob of his prideful attitude, giving him more spiritual power, not less. Even as his eyes dim with age, at the very end of the book, he delivers blessing to his grandsons, Joseph's sons Ephraim and Manasseh, and gives a charge to his twelve sons, the founders of the twelve tribes of Israel. He exercises a firm and quiet authority. In these final steps, like Jacob, we are invited to be still, yet wise, loving, and strong.

Step Nine:
Being Quiet on Purpose

controls his tongue and remains silent
—The Rule of Saint Benedict, 7:56

North American culture will not give us silence or encourage stillness. We are a famously noisy and restless people. In this step, it will be helpful to draw firm boundaries and be purposeful about maintaining them. To begin, we should imagine the world in dualistic terms. On the one side are the forces of noise and on the other the powers of silence. For a time, we make a strong decision to side with silence.

In our Christian tradition, any sense of sustained quiet is built on the foundation of a prayer practice. But once we have prayed for at least twenty minutes in the morning, we go out into a noisy world. So how do we keep silence? We need something like the beeper my friend Christopher carries with him. He is a glass artist and after years of working at the studio of the famous Seattle-based artist Dale Chihuly, he moved north to Bellingham to open his own studio. The heart of a glass studio is the furnace, which must be kept at an extremely high temperature all the time, even at night. Christopher carries a beeper that is set to go off if there is any loss of heat. He is electronically tied to the very thing that allows him to create. Similarly, we need to maintain some living connection throughout the day to our morning time of silence. One simple practice is to regularly cease all activity and look away from our task and, if we are alone, close our eyes. We need to give ourselves regular permission to be still. One solution: all smart phones come with a timer. It is a simple matter to close our doors, set the timer for five minutes, and then sit still with our eyes closed.

But by choosing silence and stillness, we must know that we are choosing the losing side. In a room full of talking people, one person being quiet makes little difference. In a room full of quiet people, one person talking or making noise makes all the difference.

Much of the practice of silence includes tactical retreats. I've discovered my car can be a relative cone of silence. I can choose not to turn on the radio, and so blow on the coals of silence and stillness left from my morning prayers. But even this is not sacrosanct. For many months, I've had a jarring experience at my local Shell station, which is the only gas station between my home and my work. A few years ago, they installed TV screens on the gas pumps and so my oasis of silence would be disrupted by an actor pretending to be my friend. "How ya' doin'? It's *good* to see ya'. Thanks for droppin' by."

There is often no way to stop such interruptions. I even asked the gas station, but the manager said TV was corporate policy. I spent a long time being irritated but slowly developed defensive tactics. There's no way to avoid the first phrase; the screen kicks into life as soon as you squeeze the handle on the nozzle. But because the TVs are designed so that they don't talk over the TVs at the nearby pumps, I can quickly take a few steps away and move myself beyond the range of talk-show news, sports and entertainment hooks, and advertising. I'm free to look at the ground or a tree and be still.

Another tactic in the battle for silence is to contribute less noise. The average American says about 16,000 words a day. Very few of us are called to the kind of radical denial that some monks promise when they take a vow of silence. Conversely, very few of us are called to speak more words on average than we already do. I have not found it easy to speak less but doing so could be a worthy goal. It is no easier than making the decision to suddenly eat less. Food diets are notoriously difficult to keep and maintain. The same is true with a diet of words.

One trick I have found useful is to remember a simple story from the early desert fathers and mothers. "It was said of Abbot Agotho that for three years he carried a stone in his mouth until he learned to be silent."[48] At times, I simply imagine that I have a stone in my mouth. I feel the texture and weight of it and make room for the imaginary stone in my mouth. If I set the stone in my mouth before I enter a room or when I am in transition from one project to another, I am more likely to hesitate before I speak, not out of fear or anxiety, but out of a respect for silence. Benedict teaches that "there are times when good words are to be left unsaid out of esteem for silence" (THE RULE OF SAINT BENEDICT, 6:2).

In the way of Benedict, every event is to be greeted first with silence. This is because if we aren't barging into a situation with pre-prepared words we are more likely to receive what is actually before us. A strong, alert silence creates a space like a womb within our hearts. We can allow the world to plant a seed in us and then from great creativity and spontaneity, speak the right next word or take the right next action. As Benedictine abbot Simon O'Donnell puts it, "The word of another is wedded to the silence of my heart, and in that union right words are born. And from that union words are given to another as a fitting gift, not as my interpretation of what is needed."[49]

The mark of a mature Christian is to confidently follow a clear call. To follow a call, we must be able to listen. To listen, we must first be quiet so that we can hear. This means not only, as in step three, sacred obedience to a vocational call, but also developing the capacity to listen in every moment of our days. One of the practices in Ignatian spirituality is a trained indifference of the will so that, in every moment, we are free to choose that thing which will bring the most glory to God. A Benedictine quality of silence can bring us to a similar place of being in the moment, quietly listening for God's subtle yet ever-present call.

Step Ten:
Being Quiet from Our Depths

not given to ready laughter

— THE RULE OF SAINT BENEDICT, 7:59

The disciplines of protecting a place of quiet and of speaking less are the outer practices. What we hope to gain is a sense of inner quiet. For Saint Benedict, there is no greater enemy of inner quiet than a tendency to laugh too easily. Throughout his *Rule* he uses two Latin words in implicit contrast: *gravitas* and *risus*. The word *gravitas* has migrated into English usage and means what you probably expect—a seriousness of purpose, a person of substance. The word captures well the affect of one who has climbed the ladder of humility. When Pope Paul VI visited the motherhouse of the Benedictines in 1964, for example, he observed the "elegant gravity of the (children) of Benedict."[50] I find that if I reflect on the character and actions of those humble people whom I most admire, "elegant gravity" captures much of what is most beautiful and compelling about them.

Gravitas also has a specific use in our understanding of silence and speech. Words that emerge from a practice of stillness and silence tend to be given their proper weight. They are not always heavy words, which the word gravity implies; instead, the few words spoken by a person with *gravitas* land in the world as they were intended to land, whether they are a light-hearted jest or a loving but serious admonition. Words emerging from silence are not flippant or ill-considered.

Risus means laughter and, according to O'Donnell, means the exact opposite of *gravitas*.

> It takes a situation or a word without giving any seriousness or appropriateness in response. Indeed, *risus* could be to sneer or mock, to be ribald or boisterous, and worse—to put oneself forward loudly without any consideration of who is speaking or what is being said.[51]

Many people find Benedict's repeated admonitions against laughter to be the least appealing part of the text of the Rule. Taken to extremes, it would seem to make monastic communities dry and humorless places. Benedict was a sober man, certainly, but his warnings against laughter have been consistently interpreted in such a way as to preserve joy, not to kill it.

Most of us have experienced the life-giving power of laughter. Some of our most joyful memories probably include laughter shared with family and friends. We know in our bones that good laughter is one of the key components of a healthy life. For a long time, a retirement home close to my church had a woman come in once a week who laughed professionally. The home would gather all the least communicative residents, those with Alzheimer's, dementia, and other assorted afflictions, in a room. The woman would begin with a little chuckle and slowly build up to a gut laugh, never using words. After a time, the entire room would be filled with the laughter of those who otherwise could no longer communicate. Laughter has the capacity to give life.

Quiet Self-Mastery

Yet laughter has its dark side, a darkness of which Benedict is acutely aware. Benedict and experience have taught that laughter has the potential to destroy community by excluding and belittling others either intentionally or unintentionally. If we are called to be in community with people very different from ourselves, these differences will inevitably cause tension and discomfort. We must be very careful not to relieve our own anxieties and fears by laughing at or about others.

Laughter can also be, like rage, an expression of a sharply disruptive emotion. It is rare that our laughter emerges from a place of deep stillness or silence. More often it comes from our sharper emotions of anxiety, fear, or even the peaks of joy. I believe, as Benedict apparently does not, that laughter has a good and healthy place in a well-rounded Christian life. But, like Benedict, I believe it is essential to be aware of the cruel potential in thoughtless laughter. As a goal, a more appropriate expression of the steady joy of a mature Christian is a kind of angelic smile. As the figure of Dante travels through the celestial spheres in the *Paradiso*, the last part of the *Divine Comedy*, the souls he encounters bear smiles that are both warm and dazzling. One soul tells him that in God's will is their peace, and the smiles are the expressive confirmation of their peaceful joy.[52] There's a famous sculpture of a smiling angel at the front portal of the Reims Cathedral in France. The angel has a smile so compelling and mysterious that it always seems to evoke a knowing smile in return. Part of the mystery of her smile is the deep sense of peace, restfulness, and silence from which it seems to emerge.

Silence, a necessary source of our peace and joy, is not always easy to love. My current spiritual director, a Franciscan monk, had to go through six months of silence as a novice. He joked with me that, after a month, he felt like shooting everyone around him—and after two, he felt like shooting himself! Too much silence early on can be difficult and even demoralizing. These are the higher steps because we first have to establish good habits, achieve a proper self-perception, and have some of our sin stripped away before we can rightly perceive and love the gift of silence.

When I first arrived at St. Paul's, I introduced the practice of a full minute of silence after the sermon. At first, I could hear the discomfort. The congregation was used to perpetual movement in the worship service so the pause for stillness was disorienting. I got some complaints. But within a few months, the community settled into the new rhythm, and it is one of the most treasured parts of the service.

Several times I have led silent retreats. Every time there are people who sign up with trepidation and even fear; they have never been in silence before and are uncertain what to expect. When I lead such a retreat, I always make it clear that for much of the time, I will be in a certain room where all are invited to come in and talk should the need arise. Although the offer is always appreciated, no one has ever taken advantage of it for the purpose of merely relieving the silence. Further, the very people who express the greatest fear going into the retreat are often the ones at the end who tell me they wish the retreat had been longer. After their initial fears were allayed, they found a home in silence.

Contemporary spiritual writer Maggie Ross has said that "we harbor a homesickness for silence that we hide even from ourselves."[53] I believe this is true and that this desire is closely aligned with our often hidden hunger for God. In step four, cultivating patience, we learned to shift our sense of time to include both *kairos* and *chronos*. Here in step ten, we make a similar shift in our sense of language. We are invited to believe that silence is God's first language and the rest is only translation.

Silence is an odd word. It doesn't mean merely a lack of noise but involves a quality of stillness and concentration. Something like the land of sheer silence can be imagined if we think of one common practice for dropping into silence, which is to repeat a phrase from Psalm 46 five times, "be still… and know that I am God"—each time dropping a phrase or word.

Be still and know that I am God. Be still and know that I am. Be still and know. Be still. Be. It is like a ramp that gently leads a boat into the waters of silence.

In silence we gradually return to a home from which we hardly knew we strayed. Anxious and hurtful laughter now fall away not because of some exterior command but because we have entered into a place of quiet and trust beyond anxiety and fear.

Step Eleven:
Being Quiet and Gentle

speaks gently

— The Rule of Saint Benedict, 7:60

In our struggle against the world of noise, we will need allies. Like many mediocre tennis players, the quality of my game is changed by the quality of my opponent. With a mediocre opponent, I am usually a poor to mediocre player with an occasional flash of high school varsity. When I play with a good player, an observer might actually think I know what I'm doing. Likewise, it is sensible for us to seek others who can draw us into the beautiful world of healthy silence and so help us find pathways into peace.

My teacher of silence was my first spiritual director, Brother Paul Wessinger, SSJE. When I first met Paul, I was disappointed. I had read various accounts of spiritual direction that made it sound like high adventure, wrestling with inner demons and being sent on great missions to change the world. I was hoping for a dynamic person who would help me, like the young Jacob, dream great dreams and wrestle with angels. Instead, I found a very simple-seeming old man who often asked me mundane and polite questions. Although he was always alert, he never probed.

It took me some time to realize Paul's quiet gift. The man was clear-eyed, kind, and unflappable. Although I rarely came to a stunning insight when I was with him, I always left

Quiet Self-Mastery

with a deeper sense of calm and acceptance. Paul saw me as myself and loved me despite my many flaws and blind spots. Over time, I got to know others who also knew and loved Paul. I learned that his wisdom and kindness came from many sources, not the least of which were his own interior struggles. But perhaps the greatest source of Paul's lively humility was his genuine love of silence.

Once, when in retreat, I went to the chapel a little early for evening prayer. Paul was there alone. I sat down across from him and was slowly captivated by his stillness. His head was tilted and his body was at an angle. He was looking at the floor with his mouth slightly open, in a way that reflected not vacancy but attention. We sat together in the room for about ten minutes. I was still and silent in his attentive quiet. After dinner we met for a brief session of spiritual direction, and I commented on the silence. He smiled a knowing smile and with a twinkle in his eyes, said, "Yes, isn't it wonderful?"

My own experiences of Paul were reinforced years later when I read an account of how he helped a friend. The friend wrote,

> I was in the greatest personal pain that I had ever known, the pain complicated by a deep sense of shame. It was something I felt I could not talk about, even with Paul. He was visiting us in Illinois on his way to his mother's 90th birthday celebration, staying at our home. It was a cold, rainy Sunday afternoon. He and I were alone after church, sitting by a fire. Because I could not speak of what was on my heart, I was soon silent, unable to chat about trivialities. For what seemed to me hours, Paul simply sat there in silence with me. It made me appreciate for the first time how time and space have a different value for monastics.

It also made me realize more deeply the compassion of Jesus, who like Paul can simply sit silently, being present to someone in pain and shame—present in a love deeper than words.[54]

Paul's deep gift of silence is reflected in a story about one of the great Desert Fathers. A bishop from Alexandria traveled out to the desert to receive wisdom from the great Desert Father, Abbot Pambo. When Pambo's spiritual brothers heard about the bishop's visit, they urged him to share some wise words. He replied "if he is not edified by my silence, there is no hope that he will be edified by my words."[55]

Paul was the closest I am ever likely to come to knowing a person like the Desert Fathers and Mothers.

In the last chapter I wrote that when I was going through my time of trial, I was strengthened by the realization that my life was hidden in Christ. The experience of being safe in another person's silence allows the self that is hidden in Christ, like a bunny in the bushes, to slowly, tentatively emerge so it can be seen and known. A lover of silence not only shows to the world the image of God in herself but also creates the possibility for those around her to reveal their image too.

One practice for this eleventh step, then, is to seek people who know how to hold others in loving silence. The quality of silence that heals us and builds us up is better caught than taught. It is like music. There is only so much we can know of music by reading words on a page. To understand the power of sound we must experience it live. The same is true of good silence.

We are probably more familiar with the ways silence excludes and hurts than with the ways silence heals and strengthens. We fear being given the "silent treatment." Yet in

Quiet Self-Mastery

the hands of a master like Paul, a treatment of silence is often just the right course for us to follow if our desire is to express truth and genuine love to others. Surveys have shown that only three things have consistently been able to raise people's level of happiness: drugs, meditation, and extended therapy. Therapy is, at its core, nothing other than two people having a conversation where one person is markedly less anxious than the other. By returning to our homeland of silence, anxiety melts away. In step eleven, we are not only healed but also can become healers of others, whom we invite to be safe in our silence.

As an example, consider my friend Carolyn, a leader at St. Paul's. If Paul was my teacher in silence, Carolyn has become my partner in silence. She is the chief financial officer for a large fund that supports non-profits, and she is nearing retirement. She has been on a serious spiritual quest for most of her life but only found her way to church in the last decade. She returned after reading a book called *Living Buddha, Living Christ* by the Buddhist wise man, Thich Nhat Hanh, who teaches that if you yearn for spiritual depth, you must return to the religion in which you grew up and dedicate yourself to it. Carolyn followed that advice and found St. Paul's. Within a year of arriving at our church, her oldest daughter received a diagnosis of virulent cancer, and within weeks, she was dead. The people of St. Paul's held Carolyn and her family in love and prayer and helped her through the horrifying process of losing a child.

Carolyn has told me that the last stage of her life is going to be primarily spiritual. There are at least two connected ways she expresses her desire to grow; she prays and she serves. First, building on her experience of exploring Buddhism and the discipline of meditation, she practices Centering Prayer and so has the capacity, in almost all circumstances, to be calm, attentive, and truthful. Second, she has joined me in helping to host a group of teenage moms and their children every week at our church. We share a love of order. The lives of these moms are often chaotic and uncertain. What we offer on our Friday afternoons is regularity, reliability, and some support for them when life goes seriously awry.

Carolyn and I believe that we do our best work when we faithfully show up as attentive, non-anxious people. The moms and their children have slowly learned to love and trust us just as we have learned to love and trust them. Now, if they happen to see one of us at the shopping mall, they run up to us and embrace us. One of the most important developments in our relationship happened one week when Carolyn, on an impulse, invited the moms to a moment of silence. She knew that I always have my cell phone with me and that one of my favorite apps is a meditation timer. I set the timer for whatever length of time seems appropriate. I hit start and then 30 seconds later it chimes. Some minutes after that, it chimes a second time to indicate that the time of silence has come to a close. She asked me to set the timer for a minute.

The effect was surprising and profound. The moms, who so often were distracted and disruptive, embraced the silence. They were still and quiet. Even more, the conversation that followed about the importance of the habit of reading to your children was the most mature, honest, and productive we had had up until that point. Since that week, a moment or two of silence has become a regular part of our ritual. Often, it is the moms themselves who request the time. Carolyn and

Quiet Self-Mastery

I, together, by simply being who we are and by showing up faithfully, are able to share a deep and simple connection with these teen moms. Carolyn's desire for spiritual growth has borne fruit not just in her own life, but in the lives of these teen moms. We are all safe together in our shared silence.

Step Twelve:
Being Vigilant

always manifests humility in his bearing
no less than in his heart...

— THE RULE OF SAINT BENEDICT, 7:62

If we go to a department store, we can be certain that we are being watched. Most likely, the cameras trained on us are there for security. However, there are also organizations that record and observe our behavior in order to help the store sell more products. One thing these organizations have discovered is that when we enter a store, we tend to look down and to the right. They've also found that if we touch something, we are more likely to buy it. So, corporate stores have learned to put the things they most want to sell at waist level and slightly to the right when we first walk into a store. The objects are arranged so that we are likely to first touch and then buy them. The habits of our eyes lead directly to our behavior.

In the last three steps, we have been attending to our ears and our mouths. Now, in this final step, we shift attention to attention to our eyes. In his eleventh-century book on the Twelve Steps of Humility, Bernard of Clairvaux claimed to know little of humility but much about pride, so he presents the steps in reverse order, starting with number twelve. This step, for Bernard, is the last one before paradise and so in it we experience the very moment of the Fall, when Adam and Eve

Quiet Self-Mastery

first saw the fruit and wondered. Curiosity, beginning with the eyes, was the beginning of pride and the fall.

Benedict and Bernard are both extraordinarily rigorous in their stewardship of the eyes. Benedict writes that whether a monk "sits, walks or stands, his head must be lowered and his eyes cast down."[56] Bernard characteristically looks to scripture and writes that there are only two reasons we should ever look up. One is to follow Psalm 121 where David looks to the hills for help, and the other is to follow Jesus who, in the sixth chapter of John's Gospel, looks up to the approaching crowd so that he can help them. Bernard writes, "The one did it in wretchedness, the other in mercy. Both acted blamelessly."[57]

Most of us can't be quite so rigorous. I don't know how we would drive a car or shop for food if we never looked up. Nonetheless, as with silence, we can make the beginnings of a practice. Solely on the advice of these ancient monks, I've begun trying to look to the ground more frequently. It runs against much of what I have been taught, which is to have good posture and hold my head up high. I began with brief experiments. There's a great coffee shop about two blocks from my office, and it was often my custom to take a mid-morning break to get a cup. I began my practice by trying to keep my eyes fixed on the ground for the duration of the walk there. I found it hard to do. If I didn't pay attention, my eyes would soon be up and wandering, looking at people and at whatever.

But slowly—and it has taken years—it has become more natural. More recently, I've gotten in the habit of walking to work, which takes about half an hour. I find that I naturally want to look at the ground and have lost my feeling of self-consciousness about my appearance. The benefit is that I feel like I am able to preserve a sort of gentle attentiveness to God's presence. "Where will you go when you leave yourself, O Curious one?" writes Bernard.[58]

If I am in this zone, there is a repetitive prayer I can naturally slip into. Ordinarily, I have a prayer rope, which is a bracelet-sized loop of knots with one wooden bead. My custom is to say the Jesus Prayer for each knot and the Lord's Prayer for the bead. Standard stuff.

More recently, I discovered a prayer out of the English tradition. It is from a writer named Walter Hilton who was a contemporary of both Julian of Norwich and the anonymous author of *The Cloud of Unknowing*. Hilton is less well-known than either of them but I have found him more useful. He asks that his readers imagine they are on the way to Jerusalem, which is their happy home. They can expect temptations, rough landscapes, and bandits along the way. However, they are to keep saying one thing in their hearts: "I am nothing, I have nothing, I desire one thing." In this way, the pilgrim will rapidly come to Jerusalem.[59]

For myself, I can only say these words if I have been led to a place of depth, stillness, and attention. They are too intense to be used lightly or when I am distracted with other things. If I am feeling insecure and uncertain, they sound in my mind's ear too much like sinful self-loathing. But when the times and conditions are right, the words emerge clear and strong. They hold my attention and increase in me an unselfconscious desire for God. They give me permission to release desire for or attention to anything else, focusing instead on the one thing needful. It is a taste of heaven.

The first step and the last are similar. Step one is keeping watch and step twelve is being vigilant. In both, we are called to be attentive to the truth that is before us. The difference is the depth of the truth we are able to perceive and embrace. In step one, we are beginning to allow an awareness of God to slowly seep into our lives by being serious and attentive, not flippant and withdrawn. By step twelve, the habit of attentiveness has become so ingrained that without effort and by grace we know and embrace the eternal truth of God's love, justice, mercy, and forgiveness. The journey has come full circle.

CHAPTER 7

Face to Face

At the end of the process of restoring *The Last Supper*, Barcilon optimistically wrote that "in many cases, the cleaning recaptured the volume and expressive intensity of the figures, believed to be irretrievably lost."[60] Furthermore, "the faces, burdened with grotesque features from so many restorations, again manifest a genuine expressiveness... now the faces of the apostles seem to genuinely participate in the drama of the moment, and evoke the gamut of emotional responses intended by Leonardo to Christ's revelation"[61] that one of them would betray him. On my visit, I was anxious to see if Barcilon's optimism held true for me.

As soon as I emerged from the second of the sealed chambers and into the refectory, I was struck with an intensely physical response to the figures in the painting. They were movingly and recognizably human. Their faces each registered profoundly felt emotions. These faces weren't at all like the remote faces of a Byzantine icon. In the room, they loomed like recognizable human figures capable of containing divine blessing and, in the case of Judas, hellish curse. They were ordinary people and yet, at the same time, in their dignity and in the intensity and clarity of their emotions, great human souls.

To my eyes, the restoration had freed the painting to be itself with all of the dramatic force that was still possible. With some charitable imagination, well formed from my hours of study and reflection, I could imagine what the painting must have been like originally. We will never see that painting. But what we can see is enough. For all its flaws, the painting is still a masterpiece. The twenty-two years of labor released the painting to once again be itself.

When I was standing in the room, which was originally a dining hall, it became clear to me that the painting offered a great spiritual lesson. I saw that Jesus, in his serene and sad expression and the perfect triangle of his gestures, anchors not just the field of the painting but the entire long space of the refectory. Standing there, I felt myself drawn into the drama, as though I were at the table with him. As I gazed, it was impossible to feel like an innocent bystander. I am a part of this story.

All of us who are baptized in Christ are invited to be a part of God's story. Further, when we share communion, we are invited to imagine that we, in a mysterious way, are at the table with Jesus. From God's eternal perspective, the Last Supper is a meal that has never ended. Even from a worldly perspective, it never has. Since the day that Jesus instituted the Eucharistic feast, not a week has gone by without some community, somewhere, breaking bread in his name. Now, with billions of Christians, we can be certain that in every moment of our lives people somewhere in the world are being given bread and wine with the assurance they are receiving the body and blood of Jesus.

In my tradition of The Episcopal Church, we are invited to say a prayer together after everyone in the community has had communion. We say, in part, "Send us now into the world in peace, and grant us strength and courage to love and serve you with gladness and singleness of heart" (*The Book of Common Prayer*, p. 365). Here, at the end of our journey, we can stop and reflect upon how Benedict's Twelve Steps of Humility can help us take our place in God's story and to do our work with gladness and singleness of heart.

We are human beings who are active in the world, always changing things and being changed. We are not paintings. We are truthfully even more beautiful and dignified than *The Mona Lisa* or the figures of *The Last Supper*, even when the paintings were new. As great an artist as Leonardo was, God is still greater.

We were created by God as dynamic beings and so our true image and likeness is revealed as we act. More precisely, the image of God is found in us human beings when we quietly follow the unique call that God has for us—not just in the long arc of our lives, but in the small moments and encounters that fill our days. A mature follower of Jesus is always alert and obedient to God's call in every moment. We are part of an unfolding story, and God, in God's mercy and generosity, has chosen to include us. We are not the authors; God is. Humility is precisely the virtue that allows each of us to take our assigned place in God's redemption of the whole world.

One of the most poignant stories in scripture is the account of the rich young man who comes up to Jesus, kneels before him, and asks what he must do to inherit eternal life. Jesus recites many of the Ten Commandments, which the young man claims to have followed. Mark's version continues:

> Jesus, looking at him, loved him and said, 'You lack one thing; go, sell what you own and give the money to the poor, and you will have treasure in heaven; then come follow me.' When he heard this he was shocked and went away grieving, for he had many possessions (Mark 10:21-22).

The rich young man received a call from God that was clearer than what most of us are likely to receive. Jesus looked him in the eyes, loved him, and invited him to follow. As far as we know, he did not. I wonder what would have happened if he had? Jesus promises that if we follow him, we will receive abundant life (John 10:10). So if the young man had listened to the call and obeyed, we can be certain he would have received gifts greater than all the pleasure and security given by his possessions.

One who has climbed the twelve steps of humility is unencumbered by fear or reluctance and so is radically available to the call of the present moment. She is impervious to the seductions of fame, power, and dominance. Humility enables her to say, with total freedom, "Here I am, send me." When Jesus looks her in the eye, loves her, and says, "Follow me," she goes.

The half-joking wisdom of the Benedictine tradition is that young monks are fervent but not holy, old monks are holy but not fervent, and middle-aged monks are neither holy nor fervent. A person who has climbed these twelve steps of humility, for whom the image and likeness of God are apparent to the world, is both fervent and holy. They are fervent because they are passionately pursuing the thing that God created them to do. They are holy because they are ever mindful of the peace that passes all understanding and have learned the art of praying without ceasing.

So much of this work of climbing the Steps of Humility depends on faith. We live in a culture with so many voices competing for our attention that it is easy to rest in beliefs that are pragmatic, commercial, sentimental, and agnostic toward any claims of ultimate truth with a capital T. But we are free to choose a better way.

Benedict left words on a page almost 1500 years ago to help those he lived with choose the better way each day of their lives. His words survive because generations of men and women have found that by inwardly digesting the words and images of his *Rule*, in particular these Twelve Steps, their faith was deepened, their hope strengthened, and their love expanded. Many thousands of men and women through the centuries have verified with their lives that these Twelve Steps work to produce mature followers of Jesus. Benedict's promise in the prologue was true. By following his simple *Rule* for beginners, hearts overflow with love. By taking these steps seriously ourselves and making them our own, we aren't joining a spiritual elite but a large band of spiritual pilgrims dedicated to devoting their lives to God and the service of others.

God is love, and followers of these Twelve Steps understand that the steps are nothing less than a School of Love. John teaches that perfect love casts out fear (1 John

4:18). So does perfect humility. By faithfully following this way of humility, we draw closer to God and so learn to love God, neighbor, and self. In this life, neither our love nor our humility will ever be perfect. But by faith and hope, we can continue on this reliable path toward a love greater than any we have ever asked for or imagined. Now we see in a mirror dimly. Then, we will see face to face.

A. Summary Chart:
The Twelve Steps of Humility

Chapter	Step	Meaning	Benedict
Foundational Habits: Personal	1. Keeping Watch	Stay alert like a scuba diver	"he guards himself at every moment" 7.12
	2. Desiring God Above All	Bind our excessive desires so we can focus on God	"loves not her own will nor takes pleasure in the satisfaction of her own desire" 7.31
Foundational Habits: Communal	3. Practicing Sacred Obedience	Plant ourselves in a church, become friends with the poor, and join a Discipleship Group	"obedience for the love of God" 7.34
	4. Cultivating Patience	Train our hearts to meet suffering like a confident non-violent protester	"his heart quietly embraces suffering" 7.35
The Image of God	5. Seeing the Image of God in Ourselves	Claim our own experiences of remembering God, receiving Jesus, and loving with the Holy Spirit	"a person does not conceal" 7.44
Stripping	6. Releasing Superiority	Endure in trust	"content with the lowest" 7.49
	7. Releasing Control	Embrace both God's mercy and God's judgment	"a blessing that you have humbled me so that I can learn your commandments" 7.54
	8. Releasing Autonomy	Honor our vows to God and each other with all that we are and all that we have	"does only what is endorsed by the common rule" 7.55

Quiet Self-Mastery	9. Being Quiet on Purpose	Choose silence	"controls his tongue and remains silent" 7.56
	10. Being Quiet from Our Depths	Keep silence	"not given to ready laughter" 7.59
	11. Being Quiet and Gentle	Others are safe in our silence	"speaks gently" 7.60
	12. Being Vigilant	With eyes cast down, maintain singleness of heart and pray without ceasing	"always manifests humility in his bearing no less than in his heart" 7.62

B. The Seventh Chapter of
The Rule of Saint Benedict

1 Brothers, divine Scripture calls to us saying: *Whoever exalts himself shall be humbled, and whoever humbles himself shall be exalted (Lk 14:11; 18:14)* 2. In saying this, therefore, it shows us that every exaltation is a kind of pride, 3 which the Prophet indicates he has shunned, saying *Lord, my heart is not exalted; my eyes are not lifted up and I have not walked in the ways of the great nor gone after marvels beyond me* (Ps 131:1). 4 And why? *If I had not a humble spirit, but were exalted instead, then you would treat me like a weaned child on its mother's lap* (Ps 131:2)

5 Accordingly, brothers, if we want to reach the highest summit of humility, if we desire to attain speedily that exaltation in heaven to which we climb by the humility of this present life, 6 then by our ascending actions we must set up that ladder on which Jacob in a dream saw *angels descending and ascending* (Gen 28:12). 7 Without doubt, this descent and ascent can signify only that we descend by exaltation and ascend by humility. 8 Now the ladder erected is our life on earth, and if we humble our hearts the Lord will raise it to heaven. 9 We may call our body and soul the sides of this ladder, into which our divine vocation has fitted the various steps of humility and discipline as we ascend.

10 The first step of humility, then, is that a man keeps the *fear of God* always *before his eyes* (Ps 36:2) and never forgets it. 11 He must constantly remember everything God has commanded, keeping in mind that all who despise God will burn in hell for their sins, and all who fear God have everlasting life awaiting them. 12 While he guards himself at

every moment from sins and vices of thought or tongue, of hand or foot, of self-will or bodily desire, 13 let him recall that he is always seen by God in heaven, that his actions everywhere are in God's sight and are reported by angels at every hour.

14 The Prophet indicates this to us when he shows that our thoughts are always present to God, saying: *God searches hearts and minds* (Ps 7:10); 15 again he says: *The Lord knows the thoughts of men* (Ps 94:11); 16 likewise, *From afar you know my thoughts* (Ps 139:3) and, *The thought of man shall give you praise* (Ps 76:11). 18 That he may take care to avoid sinful thoughts, the virtuous brother must always say to himself: *I shall be blameless in his sight* if *I guard myself from my own wickedness* (Ps 18:24).

19 Truly, we are forbidden to do our own will, for scripture tells us: *Turn away from your desires* (Sir 18:30). 20 And in the Prayer too we ask God that his *will be done* in us (Mt 6:10). 21 We are rightly taught not to do our own will, since we dread what Scripture says: *There are ways which men call right that in the end plunge into the depths of hell* (Prov 16:25). 22 Moreover, we fear what is said of those who ignore this: *They are corrupt and have become depraved in their desires* (Ps 14:1).

23 As for the desires of the body, we must believe that God is always with us, for *All my desires are known to you* (Ps 38:10), as the Prophet tells the Lord. 24 We must then be on guard against any base desire, because death is stationed near the gateway of pleasure. 25 For this reason Scripture warns us, *Pursue not your lusts* (Sir 18:30).

26 Accordingly, if *the eyes of the Lord are watching the good and the wicked* (Prov 15:3), 27 if at all times *the Lord looks down from heaven on the sons of men to see whether any*

understand and seek God (Ps 14:2); 28 and if every day the angels assigned to us report our deeds to the Lord day and night, 29 the, brothers, we must be vigilant every hour or, as the Prophet says in the psalm, God may observe us *falling* at some time into evil and *so made worthless* (Ps 14:3). 30 After sparing us for a while because he is a loving father who waits for us to improve, he may tell us later, *This you did, and I said nothing* (Ps 50:21).

31 The second step of humility is that a man loves not his own will nor takes pleasure in the satisfaction of his desires; 32 rather he shall imitate by his actions that saying of the Lord: *I have come not to do my own will, but the will of him who sent me* (Jn 6:38). 33 Similarly we read, "Consent merits punishment; constraint wins a crown."

34 The third step of humility is that a man submits to his superior in all obedience for the love of God, imitating the Lord of whom the Apostle says: *He became obedient even to death* (Phil 2:8).

35 The fourth step of humility is that in this obedience under difficult, unfavorable, or even unjust conditions, his heart quietly embraces suffering 36 and endures it without weakening or seeking escape. For Scripture has it: *Anyone who perseveres to the end will be saved* (Mt 10:22), and again, *Be brave of heart and rely on the Lord* (Ps 27:14). 38 Another passage shows how the faithful must endure everything, even contradiction, for the Lord's sake, saying in the person of those who suffer, *For your sake we are put to death continually; we are regarded as sheep marked for slaughter* (Rom 8:36; Ps 44:22). 39 They are so confident in their expectation of reward from God that they continue joyfully and say, *But in all this we overcome because of him who so greatly loved us* (Rom 8:37). 40

Elsewhere Scripture says: *O God, you have tested us, you have tried us as silver is tried by fire; you have led us into a snare, you have placed afflictions on our backs* (Ps 66:10-11). 41 Then, to show that we ought to be under a superior, it adds: *You have placed men over our heads* (Ps 66:12).

42 In truth, those who are patient amid hardships and unjust treatment are fulfilling the Lord's command: *When struck on one cheek, they turn the other; when deprived of their coat, they offer their cloak also; when pressed into service for one mile, they go two* (Mt 5:39-41). 43 With the Apostle Paul, they bear with *false brothers, endure persecution,* and *bless those who curse them* (2 Cor 11:26; 1 Cor 4:12).

44 The fifth step of humility is that a man does not conceal from his abbot any sinful thoughts entering his heart, or any wrongs committed in secret, but rather confesses them humbly. 45 Concerning this, Scripture exhorts us: *Make known your way to the Lord and hope in him* (Ps 37:5). 46 And again. *Confess to the Lord, for he is good; his mercy is forever* (Ps 106:1; Ps 118:1) 47 So too the Prophet: *To you I have acknowledged my offense; my faults I have not concealed. 48 I have said: Against myself I will report my faults to the Lord, and you have forgiven the wickedness of my heart* (Ps 32:5).

49 The sixth step of humility is that a monk is content with the lowest and most menial treatment and regards himself as a poor and worthless workman in whatever task he is given, 50 saying to himself with the Prophet: *I am insignificant and ignorant, no better than a beast before you, yet I am with you always* (Ps 73:22-23).

51 The seventh step of humility is that a man not only admits with his tongue but is also convinced in his heart that he is inferior to all and of less value, 52 humbling himself

and saying with the Prophet: *I am truly a worm, not a man, scorned by men and despised by the people* (Ps 22:7). 53 *I was exalted, then I was humbled and overwhelmed with confusion* (Ps 88:16). 54 And again, *It is a blessing that you have humbled me so that I can learn your commandments* (Ps 119: 71, 73).

55 The eighth step of humility is that a monk does only what is endorsed by the common rule of the monastery and the example set by superiors.

56 The ninth step of humility is that a monk controls his tongue and remains silent, not speaking unless asked a question, 57 for Scripture warns, *In a flood of words you will not avoid sinning* (Prov 10:19), 58 and *A talkative man goes about aimlessly on the earth* (Ps 140:12).

59 The tenth step of humility is that he is not given to ready laughter, for it is written: *Only a fool raises his voice in laughter* (Sir 21:23).

60 The eleventh step of humility is that monk speaks gently and without laughter, seriously and with becoming modesty, briefly and reasonably, but without raising his voice, 61 as it is written: "A wise man is known by his few words."

62 The twelfth step of humility is that a monk always manifests humility in his bearing no less than in his heart, so that it is evident 63 at the Work of God, in the oratory, the monastery or the garden, on a journey or in the field, or anywhere else. Whether he sits, walks or stands, his head must be bowed and his eyes cast down. 64 Judging himself always guilty on account of his sins, he should consider that he is already at the fearful judgment, 65 and constantly say in his heart what the publican in the Gospel said with downcast eyes: *Lord, I am a sinner, not worthy to look up to heaven* (Lk 18:13).

66 And with the Prophet: *I am bowed down and humbled in every way* (Ps 38:7-9; Ps 119:107).

67 Now, therefore, after ascending all these steps of humility, the monk will quickly arrive at that *perfect love* of God which *casts out fear* (1 John 4:18). 68 Through this love, all that he once performed with dread, he will now begin to observe without effort, as though naturally, from habit, 69 no longer out of fear of hell, but out of love for Christ, good habit and delight in virtue. 70 All this the Lord will by the Holy Spirit graciously manifest in his workman now cleansed of vices and sins.

C. Further Reading

Here are a handful of books and one article highly recommended for anyone wishing to go deeper in this spiritual tradition.

1. *Confessions* by Augustine

    What Benedict did in his *Rule* was to make the theology of Augustine workable and practical for a community. The two certainly share much in common. The *Confessions* is not only Augustine's most popular and accessible book, it also may be the most important book in our spiritual tradition. It is so good and so deep that it is worth rereading every year. A slow and careful reading of Book Ten, which is on the dynamics of memory, may be the deepest spiritual reading I know. I prefer the recent translation by Garry Wills (Penguin, 2006) largely because he breaks the text up into smaller sub-chapters that make it easier to pace the reading and track the flow of Augustine's stories and arguments.

2. *Where God Happens* by Rowan Williams

    The other major influence on Benedict was the wisdom and experiences of the Desert Fathers and Mothers. Benedict probably read about them through Cassian's Conferences. For most of us, the most accessible introduction will either be this book or Thomas Merton's short book *The Wisdom of the Desert*. The bulk of Williams's book is a series of lectures he gave to the John Main Series of Worldwide Contemplation. In addition to some great stories and pieces of wisdom, you get some deep and wonderful reflections from one of the world's foremost contemporary theologians.

3. *The Rule of St. Benedict*

The entire *Rule* is usually less than a hundred pages and contains a great amount of practical wisdom beyond the prologue and chapter seven (which is reprinted in the appendix above). There are a variety of good translations but a standard one is produced by The Liturgical Press, which is the publishing house of the largest Benedictine house in the United States, located in Collegeville, Minnesota.

4. *Bernard of Clairvaux: Selected Works*

Bernard is arguably Benedict's most influential follower. In the eleventh century, he became the leader of a medieval attempt to return to the letter of the *Rule* and the true spirit of Benedict. That movement became known as the Cistercians, which in turn gave birth to the Trappists. His writing is beautiful, profound, warm, intensely human, and often witty. The *Selected Works* collection from Paulist Press is the only popular anthology to include his short essay "On the Steps of Humility and Pride."

5. *A Guide to Living in the Truth* by **Michael Casey**

Casey is a contemporary Cistercian monk with a doctorate on Bernard. *A Guide to Living in the Truth* is a commentary aimed at today's monks and nuns. Some of it is academic and some of it is clearly meant for people living in monastic community, but other passages are among the finest, most incisive, and most useful spiritual writing I've ever encountered from any century. His book *Sacred Reading: The Ancient Art of Lectio Divina* is also the best guide I know of for regular, faithful, and intelligent reading of scripture.

6. **HarperCollins Bible Commentary**

Any deep encounter with this tradition requires a familiarity with scripture. But most modern readers quickly find that they are stuck trying to maneuver between a Scylla and a Charybdis. The Scylla, or rock shoal, symbolizes how difficult it is to approach the surface of scripture unaided. The Charybdis, or whirlpool, is that you can easily get sucked into the endless number of commentaries and soon find that you're spending much more time reading commentaries and other people's reflections than you are reading the text itself. If, as I would recommend, you follow Casey's lead and read scripture in the ancient way with the classic four senses of scripture, then the one volume HarperCollins Bible Commentary is the perfect middle way. I have used it for years for both my personal devotions and for the three Bible Studies I lead each week. It is consistently helpful in establishing the literal meaning of the text. It provides just enough of the cultural and literary background to give confidence, but never so much information that you don't have time left to think about the spiritual and moral applications of the text or to rest in contemplation.

7. **"Journey Inward, Outward and Forward: The Radical Vision of the Church of the Saviour"**

This reprinted magazine article from the late 1990s is still the best portrait of what I believe to be the most inspiring Christian community in the United States. The Church of the Saviour, a high-commitment ecumenical congregation, is not a monastic community, nor does it follow a Rule, exactly. However, its members are steeped in the tradition and are models of how to live as fully devoted followers of Jesus. The article can be found as a PDF on our website, therestorationproject.net. It includes an extended interview with Gordon Cosby, the co-founder, and also includes stories that clearly define the intended work of Discipleship Groups.

D. Liturgy for the Gathering of a Discipleship Group

Discipleship Groups are the basic unit of a nationwide movement called The Restoration Project. We are dedicated to nurturing mature followers of Jesus with a clear sense of their own unique call.

Churches and other Christian groups join the movement by starting Discipleship Groups and teaching formation classes, like the Basic Bible and Basic Christianity courses I describe in this book.

The movement has developed practical wisdom that includes ways to support followers in fulfilling each of seven vows in the liturgy listed below. At our gatherings and in our online community we exchange stories and ideas and otherwise inspire each other to continue to find ways to grow into mature followers of Jesus. Cards are available through Forward Movement at www.forwardmovement.org.

The following is the format to be used for Discipleship Groups:

Gathering
The people sit for a time of silence.

Opening Words
The leader reads the following words aloud.

Welcome to our Discipleship Group. May the Holy Spirit bless us and keep us during our time together. We are gathered to help each other become better followers of Jesus Christ, which happens naturally when we love him. We become better followers of Jesus by holding each other in his love and by encouraging each other to practice the disciplines he taught. Please remember that everything we say is to be held in confidence, which is one way we hold each other in love.

Members of the group read the following common disciplines.

By God's grace, I will set aside time regularly for prayer, "praying to God who is in secret" (Matthew 6:6) working toward twenty minutes a day.

By God's grace, I will praise God, offering myself and receiving God's love and blessings with the rest of my Christian community in weekly 'worship in the beauty of holiness' (Psalm 96:9)

By God's grace, I will endeavor to serve others everywhere I can, working toward giving an hour a week in service of the poor, remembering that Jesus said, "Surely as you did it to one of the least of these, you did it to me" (Matthew 25:40).

By God's grace, I will be a good steward of my money, working toward giving ten percent to the church and those in need, mindful that "where your treasure is, there your heart will be also" (Matthew 6:21)

By God's grace, I will "read, mark, learn, and inwardly digest" (The Book of Common Prayer, p. 236) the Holy Scriptures, trusting that they are "inspired by God" for my "training in righteousness" (2 Timothy 3:16) working toward knowledge of the entire book.

By God's grace, I will listen for God's call on my life, confident that I have been given a "manifestation of the Spirit for the common good" (1 Corinthians 12:7), entrusting my Discipleship Group to test and support that call.

The final discipline is read in unison.

> By God's grace we have joined ourselves to one another as this Discipleship Group, and we commit to meeting regularly for this season of our lives, believing that "if we love one another, God lives in us, and his love is perfected in us" (1 John 4:12).

Check In and/or Activity

Each person may check in for a specified time, as the group determines. Groups may choose to insert an activity such as Bible Study between Check In and the Closing Prayer and Closing Words.

Closing Prayer and Closing Words

Someone leads a closing devotion such as whichever Daily Devotion (pp 137-40 of The Book of Common Prayer) is appropriate for the meeting time of the group. The leader ends the meeting by reading aloud these Closing Words.

Please remember that what we have said in this gathering was spoken in confidence. Go in peace to love and serve the Lord.

The members respond:
Thanks be to God.

Acknowledgements

The Restoration Project is the fruit of many years. First, I'd like to thank all the churches that I have been a part of and that have influenced this book in many ways, seen and unseen. This includes Christ Church Christiana Hundred; Battell Chapel of Yale, St. Mark's Cathedral in Seattle, Washington; Christ Church Cathedral in Hartford, Connecticut; All Saints in Beverly Hills, and St. Paul's in San Rafael, both in California. The clergy and laity of each of these places have been tremendous gifts to me.

In 2002 I spent a weekend visiting The Church of the Saviour in Washington, D.C. That weekend changed my life and what I've come to learn of its ethos, only a small part I'm sure, is soaked into this book. I would especially like to thank Dick Busch and Gordon and Mary Cosby.

This book also would not be possible without the great blessing in my life of relationships with three different Anglican monastic orders, each of which has taught me a different and essential facet of the gospel. These are the Society of St. John the Evangelist in Cambridge, Massachusetts; The Order of the Holy Cross, based in West Park, New York but which I encountered in Santa Barbara, California; and the Society of St. Francis in San Francisco. I have been blessed with a tremendous spiritual director from each community. Br. Paul Wessinger, SSJE; Br. Robert Sevensky, OHC; and Br. Jude Hill, SSF have each, through their words and example, found their way into this book.

I have also been exceedingly fortunate in my intellectual and academic formation. I am deeply grateful to The Tatnall School and in particular to Gale Flynn, Marnie Barnhill, and

Rosemary Crawford; also to Yale College and in particular to Maurice Natanson, Jeff Burnett, Lynn Singer, Harry and Mannette Adams, and the Society of Orpheus and Bacchus; and finally to the Yale Divinity School and to Philip Turner, Roan Greer, and Ellen Davis.

Through the course of writing the book, there have been many friends and companions. These include my colleague group Dan Hall, Daniel Simons, Chris Rankin-Williams, Mike Kinman, Thomas Brown, Marshall Shelley, Clayton Crawley, and my Camino buddy, Scott Barker. This book has come into being at the same time as The Restoration Project community, and so I am particularly grateful for the leadership team of Suzanne Wille, Tracey Lemon, Kate Moorehead, John Ohmer, Scott Barker, Mike Kinman, and Thomas Brown. Several people have been very kind, insightful, and generous readers along the way and so special thanks go to Jude Hill, Art Greco, Kyle Thayer, Dan Hall, Chloe Martin, John Ohmer, Tracey Lemon, and Curtis Almquist. Many thanks to the team from Forward Movement for helping to bring this process to rich conclusion, Jana Reiss, Richelle Thompson, and Scott Gunn.

Finally, above all, I would like to thank my family. Thank you to all the Drakes for their kind inquiry and persistent encouragement. Thank you to my mom and dad, Vicky and Peter Martin, for more than I can write; and to my sister Elise for being such a full-on supporter and cheerleader. Thank you to Chloe, Harper, and Simon, to whom this book is dedicated. You all have been, in so many ways, the face of God to me.

— CHM

Endnotes

1 Giorgio Vasari, *Lives of the Artists*, translated by George Bull (New York: Penguin, 1965), 261.

2 Giovanni Battista Armenini, 1587 as quoted in David Alan Brown, *Leonardo's Last Supper: The Restoration* (Washington, D.C.: National Gallery of Art, 1983), 7.

3 Pinin Brambilla Barcilon and Pietro C. Marani, *Leonardo, The Last Supper* (Chicago: The University of Chicago Press, 1999), 328.

4 There is not a direct connection between Benedict's Twelve Steps of Humility and the Twelve Steps of the recovery program. However, they do bear a family resemblance. I once spent some months in long talks with a parishioner in Narcotic Anonymous making connections between the various steps. I believe this is a great avenue for further exploration.

5 Barcilon and Marani, 341-3.

6 Saint Augustine, *Confessions,* translated by Garry Wills (New York: Penguin, 2006), 87.

7 Fr. Simon O'Donnell, *The Degrees of Humility: A Virtue for Today's Christians?* (Valyermo, CA: St. Andrew's Abbey, 2002), 5.

8 There are many variations of the Jesus Prayer. *The Complete Idiot's Guide to Prayer* offers several.

9 Saint Romuald's Brief Rule is posted at the website for the new Camoldoli Hermitage in Big Sur, California. http://www.contemplation.com/community/history.html.

10 Saint Augustine, *City of God,* translated by Henry Bettenson (New York: Penguin, 2003), 637.

11 Thomas Keating, *Open Mind, Open Heart* (Amity House, 1986), 93.

12 L. Paul Jensen, *Subversive Spirituality: Transforming Mission through the Collapse of Space and Time.* (Portland, OR: Pickwick Publications, 2009). 257.

13 *The Sayings of the Desert Fathers: The Alphabetical Collection* (Cistercian Publications, 1975, Trans. Benedicta Ward, SLG), 192.

14 *The Book of Common Prayer,* 1979, 236.

15 Thomas Merton, *The Wisdom of the Desert* (New York: New Directions, 1960), 68.

16 Saint Bernard of Clairvaux, *Bernard of Clairvaux: Selected Works,* translated by Gillian R. Evans (Mahwah, NJ: Paulist Press, 1987), 137.

17 Like so much else in The Restoration Project, this term comes from Gordon Cosby. The best introduction is an ARTICLE *Journey Inward, Outward* that appeared in 2001 in the magazine for the Vineyard churches. A copy can be found on our website at therestorationproject.net.

18 Merton, 71.

19 Taylor Branch, *Parting the Waters: America in the King Years, 1954-63* (New York: Simon & Schuster, 1988), 366.

20 A description of the structure of the Psalter reading is also on the website for The Restoration Project at therestorationproject.net. It includes a sample handout. The experience has a brief break for a light meal.

21 Barcilon and Marani, 6-20.

22 The best translation available is *Saint Augustine: The Trinity* (Hyde Park, NY: New City Press, 2007, trans. Edmund Hill, OP). The notes and essays throughout the book are a necessary to aid to all non-professional readers.

23 Saint Augustine, *Augustine of Hippo: Selected Writings,* translated by Mary Clark (Mahwah, NJ: Paulist Press, 1984), 128. The passage is from Book X of the Confessions, one of the greatest texts in our tradition for slow, spiritual reading.

24 BCP, 236. This quote is taken from a collect by Thomas Cranmer used in The Episcopal Church every year in November on the Sunday before Christ the King Sunday, two Sundays before the beginning of Advent.

25 J. D. McClatchey, "Braving the Elements," *The New Yorker*, March 27, 1995. The quote is from Lord Byron's poem, "Beppo."

His heart was one of those which most enamour us,
Wax to receive and marble to retain
He was a lover of the good old school
Who still become more constant as they cool.

26 *The Rule of the Society of St. John the Evangelist* (Cambridge, MA: Cowley Publications, 1997),

27 Anne Lamott, *Traveling Mercies* (New York: Anchor Books, 1999), 49-50.

28 BCP, 427.

29 Shared at the "Come and See" weekend in GIVE PLACE in the fall of 2003.

30 Hill, 255.

31 http://www.youtube.com/watch?v=uwkU8-d1gIk.

32 Clark, 142.

33 Michael Casey, *A Guide to Living in the Truth* (Liguori, MO: Liguori/Triumph, 2001), 125.

34 Barcilon and Marani, 426-8.

35 Barcilon and Marani, 367-9.

36 *The American Heritage Dictionary* (Delta, 1992), 285.

37 Saint Anselm, *Anselm of Canterbury: The Major Works,* translated by Brian Davies and G.R. Evans (New York: Oxford University Press, 1998), 87. Note that Anselm begins his prayer with the Augustinian trinity of remembering, thinking of, and loving God. The prayer concludes with words that give us the great

summary of Anselm's whole project "faith seeking understanding."

38 Casey, 147-8.

39 Michael Casey, *Bernard of Clairvaux: Man, Monk, Mystic* (Trappist, KY: Cistercian Publications, 1991), 14.

40 Ibid., 17.

41 Evans, 255-56.

42 BCP, 424, 427.

43 BCP, 532.

44 My two pages of notes from that talk can be found on our website, therestorationproject.net. There are six elements Gordon Cosby names that he believes must be in place if any Christian community is going to have authenticity and depth. The Restoration Project movement is intended to encourage all six elements.

45 Barcilon and Marani, 363, 371.

46 Casey, *Guide*, 116.

47 Rowan Williams, *The Wound of Knowledge* (Wipf and Stock, 2000), 78. The quote appears in a chapter on Augustine called "The Clamour of the Heart." The chapter is the best single introduction to the spiritual value of Augustine that I know.

48 Merton, 30.

49 O'Donnell, 17.

50 Casey, *Guide*, 176.

51 O'Donnell, 16.

52 Dante, *Paradiso III.85*, translated by Robert and Jean Hollander (New York: Anchor Books, 2007), 69.

53 Retreat on silence at the Bishop's Ranch, Healdsburg, CA. Spring, 2009.

54 Cowley Magazine, (Cowley, Volume 31, Number 2, Easter 2005), 9.

55 Merton, 74.

56 Evans, 124.

57 Ibid, 124.

58 Ibid, 124.

59 John P.H. Clark and Rosemary Dorwood, eds., *Walter Hilton: The Scale of Perfection (Classics of Western Spirituality Series)* (Mahwah, NJ: Paulist Press, 1991), 227-28.

60 Barcilon and Marani, p. 342.

61 Ibid. p. 342.

About the Author

Christopher H Martin is the rector of St. Paul's, San Rafael, a parish in the Diocese of California where he has served since 2004. He previously served parishes in Los Angeles and Connecticut. He is the founder of The Restoration Project, a national movement of churches devoted to spiritual maturity through a balance of spiritual practices, including friendship with the poor. Other elements are structured small groups and formation classes. For sixteen years he led national gatherings for GenX and then Millennial clergy. He received both his B.A. and his M.Div. from Yale. He married his college sweetheart, and they have two boys.

Learn More about The Restoration Project at

www.therestorationproject.net